DEALING
WITH
DIFFICULT
SITUATIONS

AT WORK

LARGE PRINT

ROBERTA CAVA

Dealing with Difficult Situations

At Work

Roberta Cava

Published by Cava Consulting

105 / 3 Township Drive,

Burleigh Heads, 4220, Queensland, Australia

info@dealingwithdifficultpeople.info

Discover other titles by Roberta Cava at
www.dealingwithdifficultpeople.info

National Library of Australia
Cataloguing-in-publication data:

ISBN 978-1497387751   Large Print

BOOKS BY ROBERTA CAVA

Dealing with Difficult People;
(22 publishers – in 16 languages);

Dealing with Difficult Situations; at Work and at Home;
Dealing with Difficult Spouses and Children;
Dealing with Difficult Relatives and In-Laws;
Dealing with School Bullying;
Dealing with Workplace Bullying;
What am I going to do with the rest of my life?
Before tying the knot; Questions couples Must ask each other Before they marry!
How Women can advance in business;
Survival Skills for Supervisors and Managers;
Human Resources at its Best!
Human Resources Policies and Procedures;
Employee Handbook;
Easy Come; Hard to go; The Art of Hiring, Disciplining and Firing Employees;
Time and Stress; Today's Silent Killers;
Take Command of your Future; Make things Happen
Belly Laughs for All! Volumes 1 to 4
Wisdom of the World – The happy, sad and wise things in life
That Something Special
Retirement Village Bullies

Dealing with Difficult Situations

At Work

Table of Contents

Supervisors from Hell!
Disciplines in public
Process of feedback
The bullying boss - tantrums
Sexual harassment
Are moody- have unpredictable behaviour
Boss labels me - doesn't value or respect others' opinions
Won't back up staff
Lack of proper job description
Employee development and training
Performance appraisals
Leadership style of supervisor/manager
Do as I say - not do as I do
Lacking company policies and procedures
Poor work ethic
No development - low interest in job

Low Productivity
Staff motivators
I lead - but they won't follow!
Coffee and smoke break abuses
The overlong lunch hour
Personal phone calls
Ethnic problems
Buck-passing employees
Work avoidance
Interrupters
The 'Silent Treatment'
Difficult counselling interviews
Sick leave abusers
The alcoholic employee
Error-prone employees
Employee daydreaming
Show offs
Won't answer phone calls and emails

Chapter 3 – Difficult Situations – Colleagues and Others

Answering phone messages
Dysfunctional childhood
Serviceman gets uncivil treatment
Customer service
Colleague has tantrums
What a chauvinist!
Sarcasm

Power trips
Problem meeting participants
Why do assertive women intimidate
    some men?
Staff object to my style of management
Dating colleagues and clients
Dating mentors
Saboteur - or I'll go through the motions
    but will fight you every step of the way!
Personality clashes
Always slow
Procrastinator
Lateness
Know-it-alls
Class clowns
Gossip
Sticky-iffies (backhanded compliments)
Held back from a promotion
Freezes under pressure
Bashful
Self-beraters
Uninvolved
Sham assertive
Bootlickers
Over-committers – renegers
Stalking co-worker
Email abuses

INTRODUCTION

This book is a compilation of many of the newspaper and magazine articles I have written over the years to help others deal with difficult people and situations. If you have to deal with irate, rude, impatient, emotional, persistent or aggressive people in your business or family life - you'll likely find them in this book.

Have you started your morning feeling happy with the world, but find your day going rapidly downhill because of the difficult situations you encounter? Do you let other people or situations control what kind of day you have? Do you often feel as if you are not in control during difficult situations? It's the little annoyances that can ruin your day, so if you can handle them constructively, you're certainly ahead of the game. Learning to deal with difficult people involves learning how to manage your side of a two-way transaction. This gives the other person a chance to work with you to resolve whatever is making him or her difficult. Although you might make several attempts to change other's difficult behaviour - your chances of making a difference depend upon the receptiveness of your difficult people to change. What you do have full control over however - is your reaction to others' difficult behaviour.

Difficult people are the ones who try to:

- Make us loose our cool;
- Force us to do things we don't want to do;
- Prevent us from doing what we want or need to do; often use coercion, manipulation or other underhanded methods to get their way;
- Make us feel guilty if we don't go along with their wishes;
- Make us feel anxious, upset, frustrated, angry, depressed, jealous, inferior, defeated, sad or any other negative feeling;
- Make us do their share of the work.

People come in all shapes and sizes and they also display many kinds of behaviour. The five major kinds of behaviour are: passive, passive-resistant, assertive, indirect aggressive and aggressive.

Most people use rational tactics including logic and bargaining to show they're willing to comply or compromise to find the best solution to differences. They negotiate by giving up a little, if the other person agrees to do the same. Many find both positive and negative manipulation effective for influencing others to do what they want. Positive manipulation is good; because it helps others improve their lives. This manipulation includes giving praise, recognition and encouragement and is welcomed.

'Game players' however; use negative manipulation to acquire what they want by the use of passive resistant, indirect aggressive, aggressive or passive/aggressive behaviour. Their negative games are manipulative and dishonest and use indirect and unclear communication. Many playing games aren't even aware they're doing so and can't understand other's negative reactions. Although some may achieve a temporary sense of power, if they're caught playing games, others' trust in them vanishes.

What tactics do you use when trying to persuade someone to do something? Do you try to manipulate others by using negative manipulation? Could others object to this manipulation and result in many of the difficult situations you face? As you read the examples in this book ask yourself if you too could be guilty of any of the situations that cause such grief to others.

Throughout this book, I describe techniques that work. How do I know they work? Because over 54,000 participants world-wide have attended my ***Dealing with Difficult People*** seminars.

The contents of this book are not to be construed as being professional advice. In some instances I have quoted laws, but readers must always check their Federal and State laws to ensure that they are acting according to the laws in their areas. Any decision made by the reader as a result of reading this book, is the sole responsibility of the reader.

CHAPTER 1

DIFFICULT SITUATIONS - THE 'BOSS'

Supervisors from hell!

Who causes the most trouble and are the most difficult people to deal with in the workplace? Is it clients, colleagues, subordinates or 'the boss?'

When I first started offering my *'Dealing with Difficult People'* seminars, I assumed that 'off the wall' clients would be the most difficult group to deal with in the workplace. My second guess - was difficult colleagues. I was wrong in making those assumptions. My research has proven (confirmed by the more than 54,000 participants of my seminars) that the most difficult people faced by those in the workplace are not clients, colleagues or subordinates - but overwhelmingly, the employees' supervisors or managers!

Why is this the case? Because those who are responsible for completion of tasks by others, have not obtained proper supervisory training. Even though these people have titles such as: supervisor, foreman/woman, manager, superintendent, department head, vice president or even C.E.O. most have not received the basic training necessary to enable them to successfully supervise others. Some believe that if they have a BA or MBA degree, they have received adequate training. However, basic supervisory training is not part of most BA or MBA degree programs.

These difficult supervisors (I use the word supervisor - but this includes all the above titles) make mistakes such as:

- Discipline their staff in front of workmates or clients.
- Harass staff (either through bullying or sexual harassment).
- Have temper tantrums.
- Are moody - have unpredictable behaviour.
- Label their staff's behaviour (stupid, dumb) or make sarcastic remarks, instead of trying to correct the actual behaviour of the staff member.
- Don't value or respect others opinions (especially their subordinates).
- Don't provide the necessary training to fill the gap between the job requirements and the employee's skills.

- Are not available when their staff need their help.
- Don't give recognition for a job well done. Instead of concentrating on the 98 per cent their staff do right, they concentrate on the two per cent they do incorrectly.
- Don't back up their staff when dealing with customer complaints. (The customer complains and instead of backing their staff, they commiserate with the client and don't give their employee the opportunity to defend his or her side of the story.)
- Don't provide an up-to-date job description with key performance indicators (KPIs) and standards of performance for the tasks performed to achieve those KPIs.
- Conduct performance appraisals on staff without a proper job description upon which to base their evaluation. (If staff members don't know what's expected of them and neither does the supervisor - how do supervisors have the audacity to attempt an evaluation on how well their employees performed their duties?)
- Use the same leadership style on all staff members, even though a different leadership style is required. (Some need

step-by-step instructions - others just need an outline of what is required to complete the task - Theory X vs. Theory Y management styles).

- Have one set of company rules for staff - another for themselves (do as I say - not do as I do). They bend the rules when clients go over the head of front-line staff, causing embarrassment for staff member.
- Don't provide policy and procedure or employee manuals that outline the company rules and regulations for all staff.
- Have poor work ethic.
- Do nothing to improve the employee's interest in their jobs (lack of development).
- Won't listen to their staff's suggestions about better ways to complete tasks.
- Have a negative *'That will never work'* attitude toward changes suggested by their staff.
- Are perfectionists and expect everything to be done perfectly.
- Are workaholics and expect their staff to be the same.
- Use authoritarian management style, which just results in resistance from staff.

- Don't step in to resolve personality conflicts between staff.
- Abuse their position power.
- Don't know how to handle the problems that occur when promoted into a position where they're supervising former peers.
- Upper management have not given these supervisors the full responsibility to perform their duties properly (i.e.: Delegate and check staff's work, complete performance appraisals on employees reporting to them, discipline employees as required and preferably hire their own staff).
- If staff member's behaviour requires correction, the supervisor either ignores the issue (hoping it will go away) or bungles the disciplinary interview that results in retaliation - rather than a needed change in the employee's behaviour.
- Show favouritism to 'pet employees' (socialise with only one or two of their staff) or show bias (either gender or race related) towards staff members.
- Poor role models.
- Don't know how to manage their time and become a bottleneck to productivity of their employees. Staff either don't have enough

to do or are kept in a panic to complete last-minute assignments.

- Allow nepotism with all its unique problems.
- Don't keep promises.
- Too immature for a supervisory role - use poor judgement when making decisions.
- Are wishy washy - can't say *'No'* to requests, so overload staff with assignments.
- Bring personal problems into the workplace.
- Promoted too soon - did not receive proper training to fulfil the obligations of a supervisory/management position.

If this describes the actions of your supervisors or managers - seriously consider providing them with the necessary tools they need to do their jobs properly. Will this take a long time and cost too much? No - learning the basics of supervision won't involve as much time as you might expect - and look at the rewards - an effective, productive environment and highly motivated staff!

Here are some examples of these afore-mentioned problems:

Disciplines in public

'My boss has a habit of disciplining his staff in front of clients and co-workers. This happened to me last week and I'm still seething. It's affecting my work and I can't change how I feel until I do something about this. But what do I do to make sure it won't happen again?'

This is an example of bullying so, before you do anything about this situation; prepare yourself for the eventuality that things might get worse before they get better. Check your company policies and procedures manuals to learn how bullying is handled in your company. Document what happened to you and when it happened. Talk privately with your supervisor using feedback to let him or her know how the behaviour has affected you.

Say, *'I have a problem and I need your help in solving it. I'd like to talk to you about something that's affecting my productivity. Last week you disciplined me in front of clients and colleagues. I found this very demoralising and embarrassing. I'd like to request that if you need to correct my behaviour in the future, that you do so in private, where your comments won't be overheard.'* Then show him/her the company policy relating to bullying.

The three steps in the process of feedback are as follows:

PROCESS OF FEEDBACK

a) Describe the problem or situation to the person causing the difficulty. Give examples.

b) Define what feelings or reactions their behaviour causes you (sadness, anger, anxiety, hurt or upset).

c) Suggest a solution or ask them to provide one.

The Problem: *'Last week you disciplined me in front of clients and my colleagues'*

Your feelings or reactions: *'I found this very demoralising and embarrassing.'*

The solution: *'If you need to correct my behaviour in the future, that you do so in private, where your comments won't be overheard.'*

If the supervisor refuses to change and continues to discipline you in public, go higher up the chain of command. Here are the steps to take:

1. If this is the supervisor's normal behaviour with all his/her staff, have a meeting with

the affected staff and ask whether they're willing to complain as well. If they agree that they too want the behaviour to stop, have them write down their complaints and sign the complaints (so they won't back out later). They would include details of what happened to them:

    a) What was said?

    b) When it happened;

    c) Who was involved?

    d) Damage to customer relations;

    e) Loss of productivity; and

    f) What has been done so far to try to stop the unacceptable behaviour?

2. Ask for a meeting with the supervisor. All complainants will attend and discuss your collective complaints.

3. If the supervisor doesn't listen or change his/her behaviour - as a group go to the supervisor's boss or to your Human Resources representative with your complaints. Identify your supervisor's actions as bullying and ask them to ensure that the bullying won't continue.

4. If your boss's boss and the Human Resources representatives don't (or won't)

solve the problem, ask for a transfer to another department away from the bully.

5. You may decide bite the bullet and take the next step and take your boss to court for bullying.

6. As a last resort you may have to leave for greener pastures elsewhere. When you feel your boss has removed all the pride and pleasure you get from your work - it's time to leave.

The bullying boss - Tantrums

'My boss is a tyrant and a bully. He even has temper tantrums. You'd think we were on a football field the way he treats his employees. He disciplines in public, hollers at employees, belittles staff and is patronising and chauvinistic towards women. He's hated, rather than respected, by the entire staff. How should I deal with him?'

Bullying is a learned behaviour and unless it's stopped when they're children, this behaviour can become a way of life. Bullying at any level is a play on power and is unacceptable everywhere in society. And when the victim complains about the bullying, they're often labelled a 'woos' or a 'sissy' by the bully. How dare these bullies try to make their victims feel guilty when they're the ones who are in the wrong! Bullies are cowards who don't play fair. They use their power (be it perceived or real) to lord it over others and desperately need anger management.

Unfortunately, in Australia the bullying laws are still in their infancy and there is little legal protection for workers. If workers do take the bully to court, they face hefty legal bills with no assurance that they will be reimbursed for those expenses. Many just throw up their hands, leave the company and learn from the experience - and the bully gets off again. This is the new millennium and yet some companies are still operating with cavemen/women mentalities. I've witnessed bullying in the workplace so often that I've come to believe that this draconian style of behaviour is not only tolerated, but seems to be the norm, rather than the exception in Australian companies. But is that any excuse for not stopping this unacceptable behaviour?

Some companies have policies on how to deal with bullying but don't follow-through and protect their workers against it. Hence the employee is forced to take it to court. Victorian laws are making a stab at dealing with this unacceptable behaviour but these changes fall short of the mark by insisting that bullying must be repetitive and ongoing. To the victim - one incident of bullying is enough and should have all the protection of the law to deal with it. There should be zero tolerance to bullying - by society, companies and the law.

If you've already talked to your boss about how repulsed you are by his/her bullying and nothing has changed - you have no choice but to go over his head. However, be prepared - because even his/her superiors might do nothing to stop the bullying. You may have to leave your employment and look for work elsewhere (with no guarantee that you won't run into it in the new company). The other alternative is to prepare for a lengthy and costly legal battle in the courts. It's your choice.

Now how to deal with the tantrums. Don't try to stop him in mid-stream of his tantrum. Simply listen and force yourself not to be affected by the anger and frustration he's trying to thrust upon you. When he finally finishes his tirade say, *'I can see you're angry about this. Why don't I give you a chance to calm down – then we can discuss this issue.'*

Then walk away. If he continues to behave in this manner say, *'I'm very uncomfortable being around you when you're out of control. This is unacceptable behaviour and is a form of harassment and bullying. When you've calmed down, I'll be glad to discuss this rationally with you.'*

Make sure you document each incident where his behaviour is unacceptable (having a witness helps) and either go to his superior or to your Human Resources representative to initiate charges of harassment.

Sexual harassment

'Our company doesn't have a sexual harassment policy. My boss is constantly telling dirty jokes at work, but I don't have any guidelines to follow so I can deal with it.'

Organisations have a responsibility to ensure the workplace is free from harassment. Sexual harassment is a term covering unwelcome sexual behaviour and is unlawful, direct discrimination on the ground of sex. Co-workers, as well as superiors may be responsible and charged for acts of sexual harassment.

A complaint of sexual harassment does not necessarily mean that sexual harassment has actually taken place. Organisations have been charged with reverse discrimination. This happens when employees don't receive merited promotions and bonuses. Instead, a workmate receives them in return for sexual favours given to a supervisor.

No longer can others in positions of power 'look the other way' and ignore that sexual harassment is occurring. For instance, if I'm a supervisor and do nothing when I see another person sexually harassing an employee, it's believed that I've condoned the action. If the employee knows that I saw or know about the situation and do nothing, s/he can charge both the offender and the witnessing supervisor (me) with sexual harassment.

Each incident in itself may be relatively minor, but if continued over a prolonged period, can be very stressful to the victim. Harassment can produce a hostile work environment that can adversely affect the terms and conditions of employment and make it impossible for the person to continue employment. Sexual harassment amounts to unlawful sex discrimination if an employee is obliged to continue to work in an environment which is generally hostile demeaning or intimidating.

In Australia, it's been established that most sex discrimination is against women. An employer has a legal responsibility to ensure that there are no policies or practices operating within an organisation that directly or indirectly discriminate against women. An employer can be vicariously liable for the actions of an employee even if the employer was unaware of the actual actions of the employee. If your company doesn't have a sexual harassment policy - insist that they prepare one and make it available to all staff members. Many companies have sexual harassment advisors.

Research shows that seventy to eighty per cent of women have experienced one or more forms of sexual harassment while working. Fifty-two per cent of them lost a job because of it. This is criminal and needs swift action to eliminate such future harassment.

It's important to take steps to prevent sexual harassment in the workplace. Line management needs information about what harassment is and how to receive, investigate and resolve complaints. It's also essential that managers are aware of their responsibilities and the organisation's policy on sexual harassment.

If you believe you have been sexually harassed, it's up to you to check your State Harassment laws. Should you be the object of sexual harassment you should:

1. Tell the person that you object to whatever s/he's doing or saying. *Let him or her know you really mean it!* If necessary, explain that his/her behaviour is a form of sexual harassment and you expect it to stop immediately. Record everything that happens - date, time, events, witnesses, etc. Recognise that you're probably not the only one who's been sexually harassed by this person. Find out if there are others so you can lodge a group complaint.

2. If the person does the same thing (or something similar) again, repeat your earlier objections. Back this up with a written letter or e-mail. Relate to your earlier verbal complaints. State only the facts, not assumptions. Make at least four copies of this letter. Send one copy to the offending person; one to his or her supervisor, your supervisor (and the Chief Executive Officer of your company if you

think it's appropriate). Keep one copy for your records

3. If the behaviour continues or the company or union has not dealt with it, lodge a formal complaint with your local Equal Employment Opportunities Commission. When in doubt, call your local E.E.O. office and talk to a trained counsellor. If the situation involves physical assault, involve the police by lodging a sexual assault charge.

Note: If the first incident is serious enough, object verbally, send a letter (with copies to applicable parties) and lodge a formal complaint with the Equal Employment Opportunities Commission. *See Chapter 6 for more on this topic.*

Are moody, have unpredictable behaviour

'I can never predict what kind of day I'll have because of my boss's moods and unpredictable behaviour. How can someone with that kind of temperament be in a position of power? Because she's my boss - I need to know how I should deal with the behaviour.'

Most moody people are very immature, have low self-esteem and many feel they have to take every affront personally. Follow above instructions on feedback and start documenting her behaviour in case you decide to take further action.

Boss labels me doesn't value or respect others' opinions

'My boss is hypercritical of my work and uses labels to describe my behaviour. He uses such words as 'stupid' and 'dumb' to describe my behaviour. On my performance appraisal he said he didn't like my 'attitude.' How can I get him to concentrate on the 98% of the work I do right - instead of labelling me and concentrating on the 2% I do wrong?'

The boss who labels employees (rather than deal with their behaviour) is bound to de-motivate his or her staff. Talk to your supervisor privately. Say, *'I have a problem and I need your help in solving it. On my performance appraisal, you put down that you didn't like my attitude, but when I asked for specifics you refused to give them to me. And the last few times you've corrected my work you've said that I was 'stupid' and 'dumb.' I'm upset that you've given me those labels and I don't know how to improve my performance or what you really want from me.*

I'd like to go back to the comment from my performance appraisal about my 'attitude. What did I do wrong that you objected to?'

Her supervisor replied, *'Well, you were rude to Mrs. Brown.'* (Rude is another label that does not discuss her behaviour.)

'What specifically did I say to Mrs. Brown that was rude?'

'You told her that you had better things to do with your time other than listen to her constant complaints.'

Now the employee knows what is wrong with her 'attitude' and can change her behaviour accordingly.

The employee did the same with the other two labels and was able to determine the exact behaviour that was not suitable. Only then did she have something she could deal with and change.

At a later meeting with her supervisor where he complimented her on a task well done, she replied, *'Thanks for the compliment. I have to admit that I'm so used to hearing about the things I do wrong that it's a pleasure to receive confirmation about the things I've done right.'*

Lack of proper job descriptions

'My company doesn't think it's important that we have proper job descriptions. Mine just generalise in a paragraph what I am supposed to do. I'd like to have a better one, but don't know how I should go about it.'

Many companies use position descriptions that are disgustingly inadequate and don't include the essential information needed in today's workplace. Some only have a paragraph describing what the person does and others go a bit further to include Key Performance Indicators (KPIs), so believe their job descriptions are adequate. This is not enough. In addition to other pertinent information, a proper job description includes the following.

- A general description of what the person does (in paragraph form),
- A list of Key Performance Indicators.
- Under each KPI is a list of the tasks that are performed to ensure that the KPI is reached.
- Each task includes benchmarks or standards of performance that are measurable (rather than subjective). These measures include quality, quantity, time and can include cost if relevant.

Use the following to convince your company why the above type of position description is essential for the smooth running of the company:

- It's the primary tool to determine qualifications for recruiting new employees.
- It's an excellent training tool to compare an employee's capabilities against those required by the position allowing the company to determine the required training to fill that gap.
- Many government training grants to companies require a detailed job description so they can determine what is required of employees compared to their present level of knowledge and ability.
- Both the employee and employer know exactly what the employee is to do and the employee's performance can be measured against clear written objectives.
- Duties do not 'fall through the cracks' and eliminates the expression, *'I didn't know I was responsible for that!'*
- Morale of employees normally rises 100% when it's clear what their employers expect from them.

- Company performance appraisals will be based on objective, rather than subjective measures. There are no surprises at performance appraisal time, because it's clear to both the employee and their supervisor exactly what is expected of the employee.

- If it becomes necessary for a supervisor to correct an employee's behaviour, it can be done based on objective (rather than subjective) reasons. Should the employee be terminated, the employer can show exactly what standards of performance were not met by the employee and the documentation to prove that the employee had an opportunity to improve his or her behaviour or performance.

- It's a vital tool for manpower planning that helps determine the gaps between the employees' skills and abilities and those required to fill their next promotional position.

Employee development and training

'I've been trying to get ahead in my organisation but find that the men are given training and the women are not. I've made sure the training department and my boss know

that I want to get ahead and am interested in relevant training - but I'm still overlooked. I've asked for training on my past three performance appraisals, but still no training. What do I do next?'

This could be a case of sexual discrimination. Many organisations offer a variety of on-the-job training for their employees, but frequently, women are denied access to these training courses. Their managers make incorrect or stereotypical assumptions about the working patterns of women and the number of years women intend to remain in the workforce. These assumptions are applied to all female employees - regardless of the actual job performance or career ambitions of individual women. Consequently, the organisation may not provide the information or facilities for these women to participate in training programs.

Your first step is to establish an Affirmative Action Program in your organisation. Contact the EEO (Equal Employment Opportunities) representatives in your area to assist in setting up such a program. This program will assess the skills, qualifications and ambitions of women employees so their training needs are realistically identified and will outline the employer's responsibility in providing equitable training opportunities for both male and female employees.

In assessing the training opportunities for women within the organisation, the following factors should be examined:

1. How is information on internal training courses made available throughout the organisation?
2. Is information on the content of the training courses and the potential benefit it may provide to the career path of individual employees easily available to all employees?
3. Are supervisors or others who are responsible for the selection of employees to attend training courses fully aware of the organisations' Affirmative Action program and the need to fully utilise all the talents and skills available to the organisation?
4. Are all employees actively encouraged by management to use all opportunities for training and development when they arise?
5. Are training courses conducted in convenient locations to ensure that employees with childcare or domestic

responsibilities are not automatically precluded from nomination and selection?

6. Are employees encouraged to self-nominate for courses that they believe will be of benefit to their job opportunities, rather than waiting for supervisors to nominate them?

Won't back up staff

'My boss always takes the clients' side when they complain about something I've done. I don't condone the 'the customer's always right' philosophy. They're often wrong or see things only from their point of view. For once, I'd like the opportunity of giving my point of view!'

When your supervisor receives a client complaint, the first thing s/he should say to the client is, *'Let me investigate this and I'll get back to you.'* The supervisor mediates between what the client believes and what the staff member believes and come to a compromise or solution. Both the supervisor and the employee must understand that if the staff member caused the problem - the client deserves TLC (tender loving care) in the form of extra services or action. If the employee is right, the supervisor must defend his/her side of the issue and explain to the client what they can do about solving his/her complaint. This often involves suggesting two or three alternatives that will solve the client's problem.

Performance Appraisals

'My company doesn't have regular performance appraisals. My last one was two years ago. How can I convince my supervisor that I should have one?'

How often should performance appraisals be conducted? There's quite a bit of flexibility here, depending upon the needs of the position. The recommended times are: Shortly after the employee is hired, the first part of the probationary performance appraisal (which lists the expectations) is completed.

Two weeks *before* the employee's probationary performance appraisal period is over - the performance appraisal meeting is held. This is the time when the supervisor makes a decision about whether the employee will be accepted by the company as a permanent employee. If the employee is accepted as a permanent employee, a new performance appraisal is started for the next evaluation period.

There are two methods of determining the employee's yearly performance appraisal thereafter: It can be held on the anniversary date of when the employee started with the company; or it could be held once a year at the same time for all employees.

Some companies have bi-yearly performance appraisals. Many companies do performance appraisals before and after every special project the staff member completes regardless of the time frame of the project. The company must decide which method is best to meet their staff's individual needs.

Performance appraisal systems that evaluate such subjective things as judgement, initiative, attitude or interpersonal skills are not fair appraisal systems and should be replaced.

There are many advantages of doing regular performance appraisals:

- Putting things down on paper makes people more specific about what they expect.
- It allows the staff member to take part in setting standards they feel they can meet.

- Makes people more productive and motivated to do a good job.
- New ideas and methods for completing tasks can be discussed and encouraged.
- Keeps people from being buried or lost in the system.
- The 'good guys' or high achievers don't get passed over.
- The 'bad guys' or low achievers and those using unacceptable behaviour, don't get to hide.
- They improve communication between supervisor and staff members. The more the employee is involved in setting his or her own standards, the more likely s/he will react positively. Employees are often their own worst critics, so should not be allowed to set unrealistic standards of performance.

If the employee doesn't measure up – s/he knows s/he's failed <u>before</u> review date. There are no surprises at performance appraisal time.

'Even though I supervise a staff of four, my manager insists on doing my staff's performance appraisals. I think this should be one of my responsibilities as a supervisor.'

Supervisors have many responsibilities, including delegating and correcting work, conducting performance appraisals and disciplining staff that report to the position. Unfortunately many are given the title 'supervisor' but not given the authority to carry out their duties. I believe that the title 'Lead Hand' should be abolished because many just have two responsibilities - that of delegating and checking work.

Unless those who are responsible for supervising others have all four major responsibilities, their company is setting them up to fail. Supervisors should also discipline their staff (up to termination when experts step in) and do performance appraisals on all staff who report to them. A desired additional responsibility should be hiring their own staff (after the company Human Resource department or recruitment firm has chosen a short-list of suitable candidates). This way the supervisor is ensured that the candidate is in sync with both him/her and the existing staff.

Leadership style of supervisor/manager

'My boss must think I'm daft because he treats me as if I'm ten years old. I have been in the

workplace for ten years and don't need to be told step-by-step how to do everything. I work in a very creative field and am creative myself. How do I let my boss know that all he has to do is explain what he wants to achieve and let me do it?'

There are many leadership styles in management - each suitable for different situations and personalities. It sounds as if you're the kind of person who needs lots of 'rope' and loose supervision. Your supervisor is leading you with a style that's more suitable to someone who has an absolute need to know exactly what steps s/he needs to take to accomplish a task. Let your boss know the kind of leadership you need from him.

You might start by saying, *'I'd like more freedom when accomplishing my tasks. I'm a creative person and usually can visualise what you want and will ask questions to clarify my picture of that. I'm uncomfortable with step-by-step instructions - and like to use my own resources to do tasks. Would you feel comfortable giving me that leeway?'*

Other employees may not feel comfortable unless they receive detailed instructions on how to complete tasks. They usually love routine and are knocked off-balance when changes occur. You on the other hand, love variety and will seldom do a task the same way twice. You're probably entrepreneurial and can see all kinds of ways things can be improved. If your employer doesn't allow you to use your creative juices, you'll likely go elsewhere.

Do as I say - Not do as I do

'The other day I spent half an hour explaining to a client why I couldn't do something for her because of a company regulation. She decided to go over my head to my boss. My boss gave into her. On her way out of the store the client made a point of letting me know what had occurred. There seem to be two sets of rules in our company - one for front-line staff and another for the supervisors!'

Rules and regulations of a company <u>must</u> be adhered to by <u>all</u> employees - including supervisors. Talk to your supervisor and go over his/her head if necessary to confirm company rules and regulations. Start by speaking to your supervisor,

'I have a problem and I need your help in solving it. I was upset yesterday after I'd spent half an hour explaining to Mrs Smith that I

couldn't do what she wanted me to do because of a company regulation. As you know, she went over my head to you - and she made a point of letting me know that you let her away with it. Can you imagine how I felt when she made a point of telling me that? I need to know whether this is a rule or not so, I won't have the same thing happen in the future.'

Lacking company policies and procedures

'My boss called me into the office last week to let me know that I had broken a company rule. I didn't even know about the rule! She told me that it was 'standard practice' in her industry. Shouldn't there be some kind of list of company rules and regulations available to employees so this doesn't happen again?'

Progressive companies not only have detailed policy and procedure manuals, but they provide employee handbooks that explain the company rules and regulations to their staff. New employees receive a copy of this handbook on their first day of their employment and are encouraged to ask questions about the contents. Many companies have the employee sign a document stating that they have read and understand the information.

Then, if they break a company rule or regulation, they can't say *'I didn't know about that rule/regulation!'*

You might suggest to your employer that you take on the task of preparing an employee manual for your company employees. You would start with the company policy and procedures manuals and only include the information necessary for employees to understand company rules. This will also encourage your company to update the company policies and procedures as well (this should be done at least annually).

Poor work ethic

'My boss is the laziest person I know - she delegates everything to others and does nothing herself. She seems to spend most of her time at management meetings and preparing reports rather than doing any work herself. I get so mad at her when she dumps another task on my desk that I find it difficult to do a good job.'

There are two kinds of supervisors; working supervisors and those who are solely responsible for delegating tasks to others. If she's a working supervisor, she will likely be doing the same type of tasks as her staff along with her supervisory responsibilities. It sounds as if she is the second type. It may seem as if your boss is not doing her share, but if you look behind the scenes, those meetings and reports she is preparing are as much work for her as your tasks are for you.

And if you do a poor job of completing your tasks, you are not only making yourself look bad, but you're making her look bad as well. If your performance slips far enough, you will leave her no other choice but to reprimand you. Remember, your main function as an employee is to make your boss look good. Her job is to give you the tools you'll need to allow you to do this.

No development - Low interest in job

'My job is so boring - I hate coming into work every day. I do the same thing all day every day! I have few skills, so am not trained to do other things, but there must be something better I can do.'

There are two solutions to this problem. Solution One is to prepare for another kind of position where you won't be so bored. Have you had career counselling to determine the kinds of occupations you may be good at? Once you've determined this, take relevant courses in the evenings or take time off and go back to school full-time to gain the ability to enter a new field.

Your employer can supply the second solution. Many use job rotation to keep their employees motivated and happy. All rotated tasks are at the same skill level, but involve different tasks. An extra plus for the companies who use job rotation is that this practice keeps employees from daydreaming on the job or possibly having accidents if they work in a dangerous environment (such as carpentry). They can also fill a position when others are away.

Supervisor unavailable

'My supervisor says she has an 'open-door policy,' but most of the time when I need her advice to solve a problem - she's not available.'

Plan ahead and arrange a set time every day when you can speak with your supervisor. Many use first thing in the morning or just after lunch for this. Another is to leave an e-mail message or place a note on her desk outlining your problem and a time when you *must* have a resolution.

You might ask yourself whether you should be making more decisions on your own. Talk to your supervisor and establish your decision-making limits. Prepare sample questions you want to ask including how you think you should handle the problem. You might find that you had the answers all along and just needed your supervisor's approval to use your own initiative to deal with such issues. Your supervisor might be pleased with this sign of initiative or will make herself more available if she doesn't want to delegate extra authority to you.

Won't listen to my ideas

'I have many years of experience in my field, but find that my employer won't listen to my ideas even though they really work. The company's existing ways seem to take so long and cost so much! If I hear, 'it's not in the budget,' 'that won't work,' or 'we tried that before,' one more time when I make suggestions - I'm going to scream! How can I get my company to implement my ideas?'

Start by writing down the existing way of doing things. Then add the advantages and disadvantages of doing it the existing way. Do the same with your new way of doing things. Try to concentrate on the cost savings of your plan - in time and money. Because most companies are money-driven - they'll likely listen if you can prove that your way will save the company money.

Boss is a perfectionist

'My boss is a perfectionist. Everything MUST be right - or it's sent back. I'm pushed to the limit meeting deadlines, so can't spend the time required to make sure that every 'i' is dotted and 't' is crossed!'

Talk to your boss. Ask him whether he would rather have things absolutely correct and have you get behind in your work or continue meeting your deadlines but have a few minor mistakes. You may be surprised at his answer - he may not have realised what kind of pressure you're under and the deadlines you're forced to meet.

He may be a perfectionist in everything he does. This could be a compulsion that he can't or doesn't want to change. If this is the case

51

you'll have adapt, by improving your diligence by double checking your work before submitting it to him.

Workaholic boss

'My boss is a workaholic and expects her staff to be the same. I have a young family and many home responsibilities because my wife works too. On top of that, I'm taking evening courses twice a week. How can I convince her that I can't put in the extra hours she expects of me?'

At an employment interview, it's important that all prospective employees ask what hours they're expected to work and whether there is much overtime. Many companies state they want their employees to have a work/life balance, but in practice, their staff find it impossible to get their work done in the established business hours. Many are putting in sixty-hour weeks and find themselves taking work home each evening and on the weekends.

Start by discussing your dilemma with your supervisor. Outline your obligations away from work and ask her what she expects of you at work. She may not know that you're juggling things so much and give you pointers on what is and is not crucial to be done at work. You may have to put off your evening courses, if the company can't be flexible.

Supervising former peers

'I was chosen to take over the position of supervisor when my boss had a transfer. Ten of my colleagues and I applied for the position. Since starting the job, I've run into lots of resistance from those who worked the closest with me in the past. They seem to have problems accepting me as their supervisor. How can I turn things around to improve their productivity?'

Those who find themselves supervising former peers are faced with many negative feelings from their former colleagues such as:

- Jealousy/envy/anger;
- They know your weaknesses;
- Lack respect;
- Sabotage your efforts;
- Gang up on you;
- Expect favouritism or bias; and are prone to back stabbing.

If you're younger than your staff they may not give you the respect you need to get tasks completed. Or if you're a woman supervising men, your subordinates may balk at accepting a female boss (even females staff members may do this). Your supervisor should have already talked to each unsuccessful candidate to explain why s/he wasn't chosen for the position. Then on your first day as supervisor, your manager would set up a meeting with your new staff to introduce you. S/he would explain to your new staff that they were expected to give you the same respect and productivity as they did to their former supervisor. S/he would then turn the meeting over to you and leave the room.

How would you start your first meeting where you were supervising former peers? Start on the right foot by acting like a supervisor. After your opening statement, add these comments, *'I'm really counting on all of you to help me make this adjustment.'* Then looking each staff member in the eye and ask, *'How about you Bill -can I count on your support?'*

Do this for each person in the room. Inevitably there will be one (or even two) who make it obvious by their body language that they're agreeing under duress. You will need to take further steps to deal with these staff members.

Also state, *'Although I've worked alongside all of you since .... I know little about your individual skills and abilities. In the next two weeks, I'll be looking over your personnel files and will have a discussion with each of you to learn your career plans and know more about your skills and abilities.'* During those meetings with the dissenters, spend time trying to smooth the waters for them. If their productivity drops, take steps to correct their behaviour.

I know you can't go back to your first day on the job as a supervisor, but you could implement these ideas so you can become the supervisor they need.

Won't Discipline Staff

'My supervisor really needs training in how to discipline staff. One of my colleagues is constantly coming in late, forcing the rest of us to cover for her. She has said nothing to correct this behaviour, but last week she called me into her office and took a strip off me for something I had done. I admit I made a mistake, but her behaviour really ticked me off. I don't mind being corrected about my

behaviour, but I don't like being treated as if I'm a criminal. It was just one mistake!'

To be effective, discipline should be aimed at changing undesirable behaviour - not at initiating retaliation. This supervisor on one hand did nothing about the late issue and over-reacted about the mistake you made. She obviously had not received training on how to discipline staff. See solution under 'Disciplines in Public.'

Manager lets staff by-pass me

'I'm a new supervisor and am running into a problem I didn't foresee. My manager is allowing my staff to bypass me and go directly to him. I think he should send them back to me so I have a chance to deal with the issues. If I run into problems - I feel it should be me going to my manager for help to solve the problem if it's required. He's delegating tasks directly to my staff that is causing serious time management difficulties. It's close to Performance Appraisal time and he's said that he will be doing the Performance Appraisals for my staff. How can I deal with this kind of behaviour?'

I'm aware that you're a female supervisor in her first supervisory position. Unfortunately many male managers feel a need to protect their female supervisors by allowing this to happen. Deal with it right away. This can't continue.

The majority of companies work under the hierarchal system where each level is responsible downward for the next level. No one is expected to infringe on the 'turf' of the other, unless serious problems surface.

Talk to your manager stating, *'I have several problems and I need your help in solving them. Yesterday Staff member #1 was stretched to the limit to meet some deadlines. I learned that you had delegated another task to him and he didn't know how to fit it in. On the other hand Staff member #2 did have time to do your task. In the future could you give the task to me and I will delegate it downward to the appropriate staff member?'*

Then add, *'When my staff come to you with problems concerning me, would you please ask them whether they have discussed the problem with me? If they haven't, could you please send them to me for a resolution to their problems?'*

'Because it is one of my responsibilities as a supervisor, I'd like to confirm with you the dates I will be conducting the Performance Appraisals for my staff.'

Authoritarian Style of Management - Abuse of Power

'I foolishly accepted a position without meeting my immediate superior. My supervisor turned out to be a domineering tyrant whose authoritarian style of management puts everyone off (that's why the last person in my position left). How do I deal with his behaviour?'

This person is only happy when the 'pecking order' is established. Domineering tyrants must be king of the mountain and anything that gets in his way - he'll crush. He'll use others to get where he wants to go via intimidation. Everything relates to power and many of these people are allowed to climb the corporate ladder because of their ruthlessness. Are they liked? Not by many - but their companies love them because they force their employees to constantly be on their toes. The hair on the back of his staff's neck will automatically rise when he's nearby and their senses will instantly be on high alert preparing them for his next intimidating move.

Speaking to these tyrants about their behaviour will not change their attitude - they don't care what you think. So the only alternative is to do some sleuthing to find out how many people have left the company because of this tyrant and the approximate cost so far in productivity, unhappy employees, absenteeism because of stress of his staff etc. and approach upper management with the facts. And even when the facts are given, some companies may not act to remove the person (see section on bullying).

Personality Clashes

'Two of my colleagues are constantly at each other's throats which makes the work environment very tense. It's got so bad that I hate to come into work - and am thinking of looking for work elsewhere. Why doesn't my supervisor step in and stop this from happening?'

Use feedback to explain your frustration to your supervisor. This might stimulate her to take action. This is another sign of poor supervision and especially for the lack of discipline given to the two staff members who are making life difficult and affecting the morale of everyone nearby. The supervisor should call them both into her office and explain her displeasure at their actions.

She would outline the behaviour she objected to by stating, *'This hostility between the two of you can't go on. It's affecting your co-workers and your work. The atmosphere is intolerable and serious. I know you don't like each other and I don't expect you to do so, but unless things change and this problem is solved, I'll have to start disciplinary procedures. I'm going to leave you two alone and want you to spend the next ten minutes discussing what you're both going to do to solve this problem. When I return, I want you to tell me what you've decided to do to solve this problem.'*

She would then leave the room and return ten minutes later. *'What have you decided?'* By this time, they should have resolved their differences. They would discuss the employee's plans to alleviate the problem and the supervisor would then ask them, *'Can I count on you to do what you say you're going to do?'*

Once they give their assurances the supervisor would add, *'I want you to know that if you revert back to your old destructive behaviour I'll have no other choice but to put written warnings on your file. Do you both understand this?'* The supervisor will have to keep a close watch on the situation and call further interviews if warranted.

If they hadn't resolved the problem by the time the supervisor returned, she would take on the role of mediator so that the underlying problems were discussed. If they refused to discuss their differences, then she'd reiterate the earlier comment, *'Unless things change and your behaviour improves, I'll have no other choice but to start disciplinary action. I'm counting on you to not make this necessary.'*

If the behaviour doesn't improve - she must follow through with the appropriate action. *The employees must know that the supervisor will not tolerate the situation remaining as it is.*

Favouritism and Bias

'My boss doesn't seem to like me because I'm of a different ethnic origin than he. On the other hand he shows distinct favouritism towards his 'pet' and allows him to get away

with things I'm disciplined for. What do I do to stop this from happening?'

Supervisors are human and have their favourites and biases - however in the workplace, this is absolutely unconscionable. All employees must be treated equally. Have others noticed this behaviour? Are they willing to speak up on your behalf? If so, you could use them to be a witness to the behaviour to back up your allegations. Once this is established, ask for a meeting with your supervisor. Take your witness with you.

State to your supervisor, *'I know that you're probably not aware of it, but you are showing discrimination and bias against me and favouritism towards Charlie. Here are some facts to back up my allegations.'* Hopefully you won't have to take this to your employee relations or Human Resources department, but be ready to do so. If your allegations are warranted, you are protected from discrimination by law.

Poor Role Model

'My boss breaks most of the rules you've mentioned and is the worst role model I have

run into. Why do companies keep these kinds of supervisors on staff?'

Read information on bullies and authoritarian style of management - because many of these bad role models are also bullies.

Can't Manage Time

'At work we're either sitting doing nothing or are rushed off our feet and it's mainly because of our supervisor. She lets things pile up and is often a bottleneck for us to get the work. This means that we often have unexpected overtime. This disrupts the plans I might have had for my evenings and weekends. How can we help our boss to be more organised?'

A boss who isn't organised is often one who has chaos in his or her department. Why not ask your boss if you could help her manage her time better. Suggest that she start a 'to do' list in the morning that identifies all the tasks he needs to finish by the end of the day. S/he would then prioritise each of these tasks into A, B, C and D tasks.

'A' tasks must be done right away, by either her or by her staff;
'B' tasks are tackled after 'A' tasks are completed;

'C' tasks are done whenever she can fit them in; and

'D' tasks usually should be ignored or thrown away.

When delegating tasks to her staff she could label each request with a coloured tag. Red means that it must be done right away (giving a deadline for completion). Orange means it must be done today and green - to be done when staff has time. This way, her staff don't have to go through their entire in-basket or e-mails to determine the priority of tasks.

Why not suggest an early morning meeting where you can discuss your day's assignments and anything you can do to get some tasks on their way (that she's hoarding on her desk to dump on you later when you're rushed)?

Nepotism

'I work in a company that encourages nepotism. It seems as if most of the people here are either related or have been able to have their personal friends hired by the company. I'm one of the few who has obtained my position because of my merit - not because of my genes or who I know. How's a person to survive this kind of environment when people

64

run in packs and outsiders aren't included in their inner circle.'

You've identified one of problems that can bring on the downfall of a company. Employees should be hired because of their abilities - not who they know or who they're related to. It's hard fighting this kind of battle and it's too bad you didn't know what you were stepping into when you accepted your position. Unless you want to spend your time alone and fighting the majority - it's far more reasonable and practical to look for work elsewhere.

Won't Keep Promises

'I've been promised that the company will implement my new way of doing a task, but I've waited for four months waiting for this to happen. I was also told that I could have my annual leave in June, now find that the supervisor has cancelled all leaves for the month of June. It seems as if she breaks her promises for no reason at all.'

Supervisors should not make promises unless they intend to keep them. In the future, try to get these promises in writing (CYA - cover your ass) and follow-through later if promises aren't kept. Keep asking your supervisor when your new way will be implemented and describe the hardship cancelling your annual leave is having on your family. When the supervisor makes promises in the future say, *'Can I count on you to do this, because I'll be very disappointed if you renege on your promise?'*

Immature Supervisor

'Even though my supervisor is in her thirties and is ten years older than me, I find that she's very immature in how she approaches her job. She gives instructions, then ten minutes later changes the way she wants to have the task completed. She gossips with her staff, tells jokes and visits with her staff to discuss family issues. Before accepting assignments for her staff she doesn't stop to think whether we can handle the extra load or not. She's very wishy-washy and seems incapable of saying 'no' to others. I don't think she has what it takes to be a supervisor.'

Some who are in their early twenties make wonderful supervisors, while others in their forties or fifties still don't have enough maturity to supervise staff. It sounds as if she hasn't had supervisory training and seems to be unsure about how she should be doing her job. You won't likely have to do anything about the situation - she will tighten the noose on herself without any help from you. Upper management will soon see that she's not the person for the position.

Why don't you prepare yourself for her downfall by getting the supervisory training yourself, so you're ready to step in when she leaves? Or why not suggest to her that you both take the training (therefore you won't set yourself up to feel guilty later if she fails).

CHAPTER 2

DIFFICULT SITUATIONS - SUBORDINATES

I hate being a supervisor!

'I didn't realise the responsibilities I accepted when I agreed to take a promotion to the position of Office Supervisor. This position wants more from me than I expected.'

Most supervisors (at some time or other) ask themselves, *'What was I doing when I accepted this position? It demands from me twice as much as I thought it would! Everyone's pulling at me - my boss from above, my staff from below and my new co-workers (other supervisors) from the side - and then there's the union! How's a person to cope?'*

If feel you're in 'over your head,' make sure you immediately take a supervisory training course. Companies that appoint an employee to a supervisory or management position without providing them with adequate training are setting the employee up to fail.

The secret to this transition is knowledge. Knowing what you're expected to do and how you should handle different situations are the keys to successful supervision. No longer are you only responsible for your own actions, but you're responsible for your staff's as well. This is the big difference between being a worker and being a supervisor. Supervisors must also be good leaders, good time managers and problem solvers, have high interpersonal skills and be able to chair meetings.

What is a Supervisor?

A supervisor is anyone who is responsible for getting work done through other people by planning organising, staffing, directing and controlling. This includes clerical supervisors, foremen, managers, executives and C.E.Os.

Supervision isn't easy - it's difficult for some to make the transition from being told what to do, to making decisions for others. It's also difficult to rely on others to complete assignments for which you (the supervisor) are held accountable.

Here are some terms that relate to supervision:

Responsibility:

These are the actual tasks that require completion by either yourself or a member of your staff.

Authority:

This means the person given the responsibility to complete the task and the authority to complete the assignment. The supervisor delegates this authority to the staff member. For example: You have given one of your staff the responsibility of ordering office supplies for your unit. The employee makes a list of what other staff members require and takes that list to the Supply Depot. The Supply Clerk refuses to fill the order and says, *'You don't have signing authority.'* You made a serious mistake, caused embarrassment to your employee and wasted valuable time because you didn't give the person the authority to complete the task.

Another supervisor asked one of his staff to go to the Human Resources Department to pick up a staff member's personnel file. Because the file was confidential, the department required written permission to release it. The employee returned without the file. So, make sure your staff has not only the responsibility (the task itself) but also the authority to fulfil the obligation.

Accountability:

Many supervisors believe that if they delegate a task to an employee, they can divorce themselves from the responsibility for that task. This is not so. There are two levels of accountability:

1. Delegated Accountability:

The supervisor gives the responsibility (task) to the employee and makes the employee accountable for the task.

2. Final Accountability:

The employee is accountable to the supervisor for the task, but the final accountability remains with the supervisor who delegated the task. Because supervisors have this final accountability, staff have the ability to make their supervisor look good or bad. That's why it's essential that supervisors have the ability to discipline staff and conduct performance appraisals when tasks have not been performed properly.

Supervisor has tantrums

'One of my supervisors has tantrums. He swears, slams down the phone, throws things at the wall and has a shouting match with

anyone within earshot. He berates his staff and disciplines them in public. My staff become very upset when they're exposed to his actions (and so do I!)

I know I have to step in to stop this from happening in the future, but I lack the management know-how to deal with a problem of this magnitude. What should I do to stop this kind of disruptive behaviour?'

How did you ever hire such a tyrant? Someone slipped up when making reference checks on the employee. This employee is using aggressive behaviour and is misusing his position of power. He has likely been doing this in his past positions as well. If you allow his behaviour to continue - you are setting your company up for a bullying or harassment charge so you must stop his behaviour - now.

Adults who still resort to temper tantrums to get their way, haven't grown up. They use tantrums, because they've learned that they get what they want if they yell and carry on. They often lack the communication skills that enable them to use tact and diplomacy to get work done through their employees. They love the control they have over others and enjoy watching everyone jump to do their bidding.

Most of them desperately need anger management counselling.

Don't wait for the next explosive episode to erupt. Call him into your office and confront him with your knowledge about his behaviour. Use facts. Relate exactly what you witnessed and heard. Then relate the repercussions his behaviour caused not only to his co-workers and staff, but to your clients who may have been within earshot. Ask him to explain why he acted the way he did.

Explain that you feel he's abusing his position of power and that his behaviour is a form of bullying and harassment. His actions are so serious that you'll be putting a written warning on his file. Recommend that he obtain counselling on how to handle his anger. Be clear about the consequences if he repeats his destructive behaviour.

There can be a positive element to this kind of dialogue. Your confrontation about his actions could start a dialogue that will make him see how destructive his behaviour is, not only to his career aspirations, but to his relationship with others as well.

If he uses this type of behaviour again, follow through with your consequences. This type of behaviour usually warrants one or two written warnings and then the person is usually terminated. Along the way it's essential that you keep detailed, factual documentation of what transpired in case he decides to take you to court and charge your company with wrongful dismissal.

Helping your employees accept change

Bill Evans had decided to upgrade his computer system to take advantage of a new computer program that would save time, effort and money. His concern was that his assistant was the kind of person who balked at every change. He wasn't looking forward to telling her about the upgraded equipment and systems he was planning to install.

When supervisors want to make changes in the methods their subordinates use to complete assignments they're often surprised by the resistance they meet. This is especially true because of the rapid changes in technology that can take considerable effort and time to put in place.

One of the main things people do when they want or have to implement a change is to dive right in and simply do it. Unfortunately, most end up running into resistance from those who are personally affected by the change. Supervisors need to be aware of the stages people go through when adjusting to change so they can help their staff make the transition as smoothly as possible. There are four major stages people go through when change is implemented:

1. *Unfreezing.* During this initial stage the employees need to give up their regular way of doing things and identify new methods. This involves breaking old habits. Detail-oriented personalities will likely resist.

2. *Changing.* The supervisor explains the new pattern of behaviour or new way of doing something. Before doing this, the supervisor should identify the advantages of the change and be prepared for resistance by determining ways to overcome those expected objections.

3. *Refreezing.* Employees' use of the new method is monitored until it becomes automatic. Supervisors must watch for die-

hards who may be determined to continue doing it the old way. This can take up to three months of constant surveillance.

4. *Commitment.* People are ready to use the new way and it becomes automatic.

Planning before implementing your change will eliminate many obstacles. Here are the steps to take when it's necessary to implement change:

1. Write down the existing way the task is performed. Be specific including the what, where, when, who and how's.
2. Identify the pros and cons (advantages and disadvantages) of doing the task the old way.
3. Write down the new way - be specific.
4. Identify the pros and cons (advantages and disadvantages) of doing the task the new way.
5. Brainstorm (alone or with others' help) to find solutions to the disadvantages of doing things the new way.
6. Anticipate and prepare for as many objections as possible. Pinpoint the objections and try to develop a plan for handling each objection or minimise its adverse affect.

7. Consider bringing up significant objections yourself, instead of waiting for others to do so. Then explain how these can be overcome.

8. Ask your employees to explain their objections in very specific terms with examples.

9. Don't be content with superficial reasons for resistance to a change. Dig until you discover the real reasons.

10. If you possibly can, work out a practical way of overcoming each objection.

11. If you're unable to overcome an objection, try to find a way to compensate for it.

12. Rally enough benefits to win the person's support and co-operation despite his/her objection.

13. Find a way to ease the person's mind, to make it less risky to go along with you, despite his/her objection.

14. With habitual or chronic objectors, introduce your idea gradually. Don't try to get immediate acceptance or compliance. If necessary, spoon-feed the idea to them, giving them a chance to gradually get used to the new idea. Their objection may be

nothing more than a delaying tactic - the person's natural resistance to change.

15. Introduce the change.
16. Follow-through to make sure that your staff don't slip back to the old way of doing things.

Bill Evans's employee will need to be assured that she will receive adequate training and will have assistance at her finger-tips should she run into problems. Most computer companies who provide new hard- and software have twenty-four hour help lines for just this kind of situation. Make sure there's plenty of time for her to make the transition from the old system to the new. She'll likely need regular reassurance from you that you're confident she'll succeed in making the transition.

Young female supervisor

'Because I have several years' experience in an office and have completed supervisory training, I've been appointed to a position as supervisor of our marketing division. I'm only twenty-seven years old and am running into resistance from women I supervise - many of whom are old enough to be my mothers. Several of them have ten or fifteen years'

experience, but I was appointed because none of them had supervisory training. Some of my staff are openly hostile to me and won't co-operate. I'd hate to start disciplining them, but I might have to because they're making me look bad. How can I deal with this kind of problem?'

In the past, most women were not considered for supervisory positions until they had many years of experience. Because women these days are becoming more educated - instead of starting their working lives in support positions, they are appointed to a first-line supervisory position. This can cause some unique problems. One is the dilemma of supervising women old enough to be their mothers.

Traditionally, society taught us that the older woman - the mother or the aunt - knows more, so therefore is to be treated with deference and respect. Switching roles is upsetting to both the young female supervisor (who's suddenly in the position of the parent) and the older female employee (who's now in the position of the child seeking approval).

Lydia, the young supervisor, soon realised that she had to clear the air with her subordinates.

She called a meeting with her staff and asked them how she could ease the transition for them. At first there was dead silence, but eventually Betty (one of the less hostile women) explained that they had all been upset when she had been hired. Most of them felt that one of them should have been promoted to the position when it became vacant.

'Do you know why that didn't occur?' asked Lydia.

No one seemed able to answer so Lydia added, *'I was appointed specifically because I've received supervisory training. Have any of you had training in that area?'*

'I was put into an acting supervisory position when my boss was away sick,' one employee replied.

'That's excellent developmentally, but unless you've had proper supervisory training, handling a supervisory job can be overwhelming. How many of you applied for a supervisory position?'

Three women replied that they had done so.

'Would you like to make certain that you're not overlooked in the future?'

There was a resounding, *'Yes!'* from all three.

'Well, let's see if we can put you into the supervisory training program. That way, you won't be overlooked in the future. I'll do everything I can to help you obtain such a position, but you'll have to do your share by performing well and obtaining the necessary training.' She added, *'I'm counting on all of you to co-operate and do your work properly.'* She then asked each staff member, *'Can I count on you to do this?'*

One employee, Julie, appeared reluctant to make a commitment to her, so Janet knew she would have to watch her performance. Soon the woman's low productivity and poor work habits made it necessary for Janet to counsel her on her behaviour. She again explained what she expected from Julie and what the consequences would be if she continued to produce sloppy reports. Unfortunately, Julie never did accept Lydia as her supervisor. She continued to produce sloppy work and eventually had to be fired.

Lydia fared better with the others. When she noticed a change in their attitude and productivity, she thanked them for their understanding and co-operation. Two of the women asked for and were given supervisory training.

Another problem that female supervisors can run into is the difference in the service provided by support staff (mainly women). In the past, most went out of their way to keep their bosses (usually male) organised, on time and comfortable. They nurtured their bosses (brought them coffee, reminded them of appointments, opened and sorted their mail). But when a woman's promoted to that same position, the nurturing may stop unless she's on top of the situation. She'll have to let her staff know that she expects the same kind of treatment given to the former male supervisor.

Women Supervising Men

'I have no trouble supervising women - but sure do when it comes to supervising men!'

Angela is a designer who supervises four male technologists. Even though she clearly explains how she wants tasks completed, the men kept doing things 'their' way. Fortunately, before accepting her position she had obtained supervisory training that prepared her to act confidently.

When one of her male subordinates refused to do a task her way (which was an act of insubordination - a serious enough infraction to have him terminated) Angela conducted a disciplinary interview. She carefully documented the interview and placed a written warning on his file that identified that his employment with the company would be terminated if a similar incident happened in the future.

If you're a woman, would you have felt confident doing this on your own if you were supervising men? If you're planning to climb the corporate ladder, it's a distinct possibility that you <u>will</u> be supervising men in the future. Make sure you're prepared to handle it.

Hired the wrong person

'Two months ago I hired an employee, but he's turned out to be completely unacceptable. How can I be sure that next time I will choose the right person?'

If recruiters, supervisors and managers don't take enough time when hiring employees, they'll find they've set themselves up for a period of misery. Problems can occur if:

- The right questions aren't asked on the interview;
- The interviewers aren't knowledgeable enough to hire competent personnel; or
- References aren't checked properly.

Companies may end up with a real loser, who instead of helping their company with production, cause more work in the long run. Have you hired someone and found that:

a) They lied on the interview about how long they'd worked for a company?
b) They told you they had more experience than they actually had?
c) They weren't able to handle the duties of the position after considerable in-house or professional training?
d) You were on a different wave-length than they and found it difficult to get them to do things your way?
e) You required a self-starter and the employee required very detailed instructions to get anything done?
f) The person who was hired to work on the front lines dealing directly with clients, doesn't have the people-skills you require?
g) They didn't fit in with the existing staff?

h) Their work ethic left much to be desired?

i) The person has a negative attitude, who gripes and complains about everything which eventually affects his/her co-workers resulting in low morale for all your staff?

j) Your company has installed a new computer system, but the new employee is unwilling or unable to pick up the new technology.

k) The person looked very presentable on the interview, but their day to day appearance leaves much to be desired even after several talks you've had with him/her.

l) The person puts things off so long (procrastinates) that project deadlines aren't met?

m) The employee is a perfectionist in everything they do, which holds up progress?

n) Employee is a know-it-all, doesn't follow directions, does things his/her own way and bucks the system?

I'm sure you've run into the above kinds of employees in your daily work situation. It's hard to evaluate people's ability to fit the needs of a particular position. Unless you've had years of experience, it can be a very intimidating experience. Proper interviewing, screening and especially reference checking of the above employees would have eliminated most of these problems. So doing things correctly *before* they're hired is crucial. If this requires recruitment interviewing skills training - make sure you obtain it so you don't hire another 'dud.'

Reference Checking

Employment application forms

The following information should be included on company employment application forms that will protect companies from being charged under the privacy act:

****

I certify that the statements made by me in this application are true and complete. I understand and agree that a false statement may disqualify me from employment or result in dismissal.

Permission is granted for {your company name} to contact my past employers for references.

Signature: _____Date: _____

****

When conducting reference checks start with the last supervisor/manager and work backwards chronologically. Contact at least two, preferably three former managers. It's best to speak with the applicant's former managers rather than someone in the former company's Human Resources Department.

Those who have worked closely with a former employee know far more about his/her work habits than the Human Resources Department personnel might know. However, if the former supervisor is not available, contact the Human Resources Department. References that are ten years or older do not normally warrant reference checks.

Problems may occur if candidates don't want to jeopardise their present position and may have been with their present employer for several years. The candidate can be asked if there is a member or former member of his/her company who would comment on his/her performance and yet not jeopardise his/her position with the company. There is considerable risk in hiring someone who will not agree to the above.

Treat all reference checks as highly confidential. They're to be kept locked away in private files - not the employee's subsequent personnel file. Former employers may hesitate to say anything that might spoil the applicant's chance of earning a livelihood, even though his/her record with them may have been poor. If former employers appear to be hedging with their answers, explain to them that the information is strictly confidential and **keep it that way**. Explain that you require their assistance in assessing the former employee honestly and without prejudice.

Make sure you identify yourself and the company when making reference checks. Start your conversation by stating *'Mr/Ms …… … … … …. has applied to us for a position and has given me permission to contact you to verify some information s/he has given us. Do you remember him/her?* Examples of the questions that can be asked when conducting a reference-checking interview are:

- Did they report to the referee?
- Dates of employment;
- Position held;
- Duties of position;
- Did applicant supervise staff?
- Salary: (be sure to distinguish between base salary and any fringe earnings);

- How did the applicant relate to peers? Subordinates? Clients? Supervisors?
- How was employee's attendance? Punctuality? General health? If unsatisfactory, why?
- How would you rate applicant's technical knowledge?
- Any problems or deficiencies?
- Quality of work?
- Quantity of work completed?
- Personal grooming;
- Dependability;
- Cooperativeness;
- Creativity (if applicable);
- What company did s/he work for before joining your company?
- What company did s/he go to after employment with your company?
- Why did applicant leave your company?
- Is there anything else you could tell me about the candidate?
- Would you re-hire?

Other questions would relate to concerns that were identified at the time of the interview and can be added to the Reference Checking Form before commencing the interview. Be sure to note the date, name, position, company name, address and phone number of the person giving the reference. End the interview by thanking the person for answering your questions.

Aggressive Worker

'One of my employees seems to have a chip on his shoulder and takes offence at every word I speak to him. He argues with every comment others make and is generally a pain in the neck. I've inherited him - I certainly wouldn't have hired him, but I'm stuck with him and have to deal with his aggressive behaviour.'

The feelings that cause an aggressive attitude in employees are deep rooted. The supervisor faces the problem of either changing them (which admittedly is difficult) or re-directing them to the advantage, not only for the company, but for the employee as well. Some job-related causes of aggressive behaviour on the part of employees could include:

1. Insecurity on the job.
2. Employee's lack of qualifications or credentials.
3. Little recognition for employee's achievements.
4. Under-utilisation of their abilities.

5. Lack of acceptance with work groups (including racial and cultural differences).

6. Failure to feel settled into their occupations. Those who don't believe they fit into their positions could become aggressive towards their immediate bosses, the company, top management, the job and fellow workers. Some effort can be made toward directing the negative attitudes of aggression toward a work-related goal if the attitude can't be changed. Techniques a supervisor might use are:

1. Show employees how their fellow workers count on their efforts and how important their jobs are to the company.

2. Make problem employees feel secure in their jobs.

3. Indicate that with their training and other qualifications, they have the capability to do more than a satisfactory job.

4. Give recognition more frequently to aggressive-tendency employees.

5. Bring them into group conversations: ask for their advice.

6. Identify their responsibilities and set performance standards.

If the supervisor's attitude indicates that s/he feels the problem employee has much to contribute to the entire group's productivity, the employee is likely to assume such a role. Most aggressive employees are very success-oriented. Their drive for recognition could cause the employee to set high goals for him/herself in order to achieve further recognition. Channelling this energy in the right direction can be a major step in the right direction for this type of employee.

Low Productivity

Dr. Daly asked how he could motivate one of his employees, a receptionist-nurse who had worked for him for three years. Her performance was quickly going downhill. She was lethargic, lacked initiative and her sense of urgency was completely missing. Because of the economic situation, he had not been able to give her a raise for over a year and the situation wasn't likely to change in the near future. What other things could he have done to motivate her to be a better performer?

Much more is involved in supervising employees than simply assigning and checking work, assessing performance and disciplining employees. Supervising people is an art that depends to a great extent on how well staff can be motivated.

Supervisors must watch for the 'Pygmalion effect' when trying to motivate staff. If a supervisor believes employees are smart, s/he will treat them that way. If a supervisor believes employees are capable of independent thought, s/he will treat them that way. Unfortunately, if the supervisor believes they are lazy, dumb or slow to pick up new ideas (or have any other undesirable attribute) s/he often treats them that way too. People respond to what they perceive is wanted from them. If supervisors expect high achievement, that's likely what they'll get. If supervisors expect low productivity, that's likely what they'll get as well.

Do you need to change your attitude towards the abilities of your staff? Are you letting the Pygmalion effect influence how you supervise your staff?

Has Dr. Daly checked to see that his employee has an accurate up-to-date job description with standards of performance for each task? She may not know what you expect from her, so this is the place to start. Talk to her to find out what she has to say about her lethargic performance. Some people are motivated by their interest in the work itself. She may be bored with her job and need stimulus to do better work. If this is the case, see if there are any of your duties you could delegate to her so she'll continue on a learning curve. If this isn't possible, job rotation is another motivator because it keeps employees from being bored with their assignments. This also has a spin-off benefit that if one employee is away sick, another is qualified to take over for the absent employees. This ensures that work does not pile up for the absent staff member.

Could your employee be having problems being accepted by her peers or could she be in the throes of a personality clash with another employee? Try to help your employees to work together as a team by giving them team projects. If the latter problem is the case, step in to stop the conflict.

Could she have concerns about the security of her position? Has it been necessary for you to cut staff or put some of your staff on part-time employment? Don't overlook the possibility that this is the reason for her lack of motivation.

Those who believe their positions are in jeopardy will often stop taking any kind of risk when performing their tasks. Many will resort to helplessness and appear to need far more direction from their supervisors. Rather than make a wrong decision, they revert to 'playing it safe' and get every new task approved by their supervisors.

Staff Motivators

Other motivators are the desire or need for:

Money: Many supervisors feel this is the only incentive that would really motivate employees. For some, this is true - but for the majority - it's not true. In others, just the opportunity of making more money can be a motivator (such as a possible promotion).

Recognition: This is probably the best motivator of all. It's very high on employees' lists for more favourable behaviour that in turn allows them to receive more recognition. A well-timed pat on the back can turn around even the most lethargic, aggressive or demanding employee. If you want even more impact, put your praise down on paper, so the recipient can save it and read it whenever s/he wishes.

Seniority: Employees receive special company benefits because of long-term employment. This could be a bigger office, more company benefits, a company car, etc. However, this can de-motivate other more conscientious or high-achieving employees who see seniority as a negative reason for recognition and more perks.

Merit System: This would make sure that employees would receive a salary in ratio to their productivity, rather than to their seniority with their company. This cuts out much of the 'deadwood' in corporations. Those who've always expected their company to protect their employment simply because they've worked for the company for a long time - fear this method.

Status: This would be the title of the position or the employee's perceived importance to the company. For instance, do you think a staff member would prefer the title Junior Clerk or Administrative Assistant? I'm sure you'll agree that Administrative Assistant sounds more important.

Challenge: The opportunity to grow, to stretch, to use their full potential is *the* motivator for many employees. The idea of winning is a definite turn-on to many who enjoy the gamble.

Competition. To those with a competitive nature (most sales types) competition is a definite turn-on to higher productivity. They thrive on the excitement of the challenge.

Security: For employees who believe their jobs are in jeopardy (or those waiting for a pending lay-off) letting them know that their job is secure (and the company is solvent) may be the only motivator they need to do a good job.

97

Security applies to other safety issues such as air pollution and smoking issues.

Lack of security: If their job is on the line because of poor productivity or behaviour, they'll likely clean up their act and produce more. This is a negative motivator, but may be the only motivator for your lazier employees or those who lack direction and goals.

Responsibility: Doing only part of the job can be a turn-off to some employees. When they have the full responsibility for the completion of a task, they feel a much higher sense of achievement. They say, *'I was in charge of that project. My boss said I did a good job.'*

Promotional Opportunities: This is a turn-on to the high achiever or someone who really wants to get ahead in a hurry. For those who are at the minimum wage level, it can be an incentive to work harder, so they can earn more money.

Training: When companies supply training to their employees, the employees feel that the company cares about them and are interested in their well-being. Companies that implement manpower planning use training to make sure their existing staff are ready for promotional opportunities. This also encourages longevity with the company. They provide for development of employees' talents and abilities and allow them to use the training on the job.

Achievement: Many companies make public announcements when their employees accomplish something unexpected. *'I'd like to congratulate Patti Smith who was able to resuscitate Mrs. Jones when she had a heart attack in our company parking lot. Congratulations Patti!'*

Awards: Companies give perfect attendance awards, sales awards, charity awards and give recognition for work above and beyond the call of duty.

Extra privileges: Employers might decide to let their employees go home when they've complete their allotted work. There are no specific hours of work - just allotted amount of work.

Additional Benefits: This could include a company car, an expense account, a corner office, their own personal assistant, company credit card, season's tickets to concerts or sporting events or the use of a condominium on the Gold Coast, etc.

Leadership style of supervisor: A good leader can motivate employees to give their best effort, simply because they respect their leader and want to do their best for him/her. In return, they want their supervisor to be proud of them.

Hours of work: Companies have implemented flex-time and find it to be a great motivator. Their early risers start at 7:00 am and leave at 3:00 pm. Late starters start work at 10:00 am and leave at 6:00 pm.

Job Sharing: This occurs when two employees share the responsibilities of one (normally full-time) position. Some split the duties with one person working in the morning, another in the afternoon. In other cases, the employees may work two days one week and three the next. It's an ideal set-up for many working mothers with young children. Salaries and benefits are also split in half.

Company Social Events: The opportunity for workers to associate with each other socially is a good motivator for some employees. This could be having a company sports team, company picnic, barbecue or other social event.

The work itself: Job rotation often reduces the boredom of repetitive tasks. There's another spin-off benefit - that of having more than one person qualified to take over the duties of a position for an employee who's on vacation or away because of illness.

Be aware that it's not possible to motivate everyone - you just *can't* motivate some people. With this type of unsatisfactory worker, start by explaining exactly what you expect of them (document your requests properly) and make sure they have a good job description. Then give them ample opportunity to improve their performance. If they refuse to conform, replace them with good workers. There are too many excellent people who are unemployed, for companies to keep foot-draggers on the payroll. They just de-motivate everyone around them.

I lead - but they won't follow!

'There's something wrong with the way I'm dealing with my staff. They seem to resist my efforts to keep things streamlined in our office. What am I doing wrong?'

Your problems could stem from the manner in which you lead your staff. Every member of your staff might have to be treated differently. For instance, one employee may need constant help from you, need step-by-step instructions and balk at any sign of changes. Another might just want you to explain the task and let them do things their own way. They'll want you to be available if they require assistance, but they don't want you to 'hover' over them while they perform their tasks.

Here are seven methods of leadership behaviour. You will likely use all seven, but most supervisors these days find that they prefer styles five, six and seven the most. The leadership styles go from boss-centred leadership to employee-centred leadership. It's up to you to decide which style suits each situation:

1. ***Supervisor makes the decision and announces it***
   In this case, the boss identifies a problem, considers alternative solutions, chooses one of them and then reports this decision to the subordinates for implementation. They may or may not give consideration to what they believe their subordinates will think or feel about the decision. In any case, they provide no opportunity for them to participate directly in the decision-making process. Coercion may or may not be used or implied. An example of this would be when a new company rule or regulation is being set into place.

2. *Supervisor sells the decision*

Here the supervisor, as before, takes responsibility for identifying the problem and arriving at a decision. However, rather than simply announcing it, they take the additional step of persuading their subordinates to accept it. In doing so, they recognise the possibility of some resistance among those who will be faced with the decision and seek to reduce this resistance by indicating, for example, what the employees have to gain from their decision. In the example given above, the supervisor would give reasons why the new rule or regulation is being implemented.

3. *Supervisor presents ideas, invites questions*

Here the boss has arrived at a decision and seeks acceptance of his/her subordinates and gives fuller explanation of the thinking and intentions of the supervisor. After presenting the ideas, questions are invited so that associates can better understand what they're trying to accomplish. This 'give and take' also enables the supervisor and the subordinates to explore more fully, the implications of the decision. The staff is invited to ask questions about the why's and wherefore's about the new rule or regulation being implemented.

4. **Supervisor presents a tentative decision subject to change**

This kind of behaviour permits the subordinates to exert some influence on the decision. The initiative for identifying and diagnosing the problem remains with the boss. Before meeting with the staff the manager has thought the problem through and arrived at a decision - but only a tentative one. Before finalising it, the supervisor presents the proposed solution for the reaction of those who will be affected by it.

The supervisor says in effect, *'I'd like to hear what you have to say about the plan that I have developed. I'd appreciate your frank reactions, but will reserve the final decision for myself.'*

5. **Supervisor presents the problem, gets suggestions and then makes the decision**

Up to this point, the boss has come before the group with a solution. Not so in this case. The subordinates now get the first chance to suggest solutions. The supervisor's initial role involves identifying the problem. The supervisor might, for example, say something of this sort: *'We're faced with a number of complaints from newspapers and the general public about our service policy. What's wrong here? What ideas do you have for coming to grips with this problem?'*

The function of the group becomes one of increasing the supervisor's range of possible solutions to the problem. The purpose is to capitalise on the knowledge and experience of those who are on the 'firing line.' From the expanded list of alternatives developed by the supervisor and the subordinates, they then select the solution that's regarded as the most promising.

6. *Supervisor defines the limits and requests the group to make a decision*

At this point, the supervisor passes to the group (possibly including themselves as a member) the right to make decisions. Before doing so, however, they define the problem to be solved and the boundaries within which the decision must be made.

An example might relate to how the staff deals with unruly children. The boss decides that this is something that should be worked on by the people involved so they can come up with a plan that would be workable for all the staff. Right now, each staff member deals with the problem independently, with little guidance or consistency with other staff members' methods. Because this is such a touchy issue, the boss decided that a policy must be written and implemented. This way his staff would feel more comfortable dealing with unruly children on company premises. At a meeting of his staff, he explains the problem and everyone is invited to brainstorm to come up with suggestions (some might be fairly hilarious). Each serious suggestion would be discussed, the pros and cons of each suggestion would be outlined and then a decision would be made by the group about which method they would use.

The same tactic could be used to implement flex-time - who wanted to work from seven to three; eight to four; or nine to five. Because the entire group is involved in making the decision, there were few grumbles after the system is put in place.

7. *Supervisor permits the group to make decisions within prescribed limits*

This represents an extreme degree of group freedom, only occasionally encountered in formal organisations, as for instance, in research groups. Here the team of managers undertakes the identification and diagnosis of a problem, develops alternative procedures to solve it and decides on one or more of these alternative solutions. The only limits directly imposed on the group by the organisation are those specified by the team's boss. However, if the team's boss participates in the decision-making process, s/he'll do so with no more authority than any other member of the group and will commit him/herself in advance to assist in implementing whatever decision the group makes.

You could use this system when one staff member wishes the rest of the staff to know important information that may affect their jobs. For instance a staff member becomes aware of changes in the company's reporting system and calls a meeting to describe it to the rest of the staff. Another staff member may call a meeting to discuss the changes that are going to be made to their filing system. Another person may be in charge of keeping track of holiday time, so calls a meeting to ask the staff when they plan on taking their annual vacation.

When I was Human Resources Manager, I used this method when I was in charge of setting up an orientation program for my company. The senior staff was invited to a meeting where they discussed what should be included in the orientation package for new employees.

Coffee and Smoke Break Abuses

'One of my technicians abuses his coffee breaks. He's away longer and longer every day and is setting a bad example for the rest of the staff. Another employee takes five minute smoke breaks every hour.'

Studies indicate that some sort of break in the work schedule increases production. Some firms permit their employees to have their coffee and snacks at their work stations or desks. No particular time is set for the break and it tends to fit into the normal flow of work. Any congregating is discouraged. Many employees will not interrupt the flow of work, either because they use the more slack moments for the snack or because frequently they don't care to have something to eat.

The second type is a work stopping time where everyone congregates in one area - a lunch room or cafeteria. Supervisors must discourage employees from slowing down in anticipation of the coffee break. At the conclusion of the break, the resumption of work must be commenced; otherwise, the fifteen minute coffee break can extend by five minutes beforehand and then at least five minutes afterward (bathroom break). The supervisory personnel should be visible immediately before and after the coffee break. They can make direct observation of abuses and encourage more productive use of time. Handing out assignments, checking on progress and other supervisory functions can be accomplished prior to and right after the break.

Despite efforts, some employees will look upon the coffee break as an opportunity to socialise and waste time. Only a conscientious effort on the part of the supervisory personnel to observe abuses and restrict excessive break activity will cause the segregation of those who occasionally abuse, from those who will consistently abuse the time allotted.

Those who smoke should know that they are given the same total time during the day as are allowed for coffee breaks. Therefore, if the coffee breaks are normally fifteen minutes in the morning and the afternoon - the person would be entitled to the same breaks during the day - but no additional time off for coffee. You'd have to make sure that the employees did not take additional time for breaks.

The Overlong Lunch Hour

'Marty, my accountant constantly takes extra time during his lunch hour. What should I say to him?'

Abuses such as washing up and preparing for the break and getting organised after the actual break, adds up to a lot of lost production time. In addition, the actual time off the premises or at the cafeteria seems to grow when no effort is applied to monitor this abuse. While a manager may close his/her eyes to the lost time as being of small consequence, the few employees who get away with the extended lunches will generally cause adverse affects on employee morale. It's always better not to hedge. Get to the issue - no games. The supervisor should confront the person openly and tell him/her that they are abusing the lunch hour privileges.

After lunch, the supervisor should be available to assess late employees. Several discipline possibilities exist, including docking or lateness, minimising overtime and changing the hour for lunch for some of the employees who are problems.

Start by stating, *'Marty, I see you're still having difficulty getting back on the job at one o'clock. Starting tomorrow, let's try having your lunch hour start at twelve-thirty and see if that's better.'*

Personal phone calls

'One of my staff - Shelly - spends far too much time making or receiving personal phone calls.'

To supervisors, nothing can be as annoying as watching an employee receiving or initiating an excessive number of personal telephone calls. It's not just that the company's phone lines are being tied up, but their workflow is being interrupted. An employee's personal calls should be held to a minimum. After all, s/he is at a place of business and personal requirements should wait until breaks or after work.

You might say to the phone abuser, *'Sally, when you use company time to conduct personal business, whether it is a telephone call, gossiping or just discussing what you did on the weekend, you're using part of my office budget without anything productive coming back.'*

You might also:

1. Ask her to advise her friends and relatives about the company policy. Reserving the phones for important or emergency calls may not eliminate the frivolous calls entirely, but it will make fair minded employees follow the rules.

2. If you don't have voice mail, have the receptionist ask an incoming caller for his or her name and say, *'Can you tell me the reason for your call or is this a personal call?'* Nothing further needs to be ventured by the receptionist. The question may be enough to embarrass the caller without being too nosy. Such a question tends to reduce the calls and their duration. Or the receptionist might keep track of such calls for one or two days and submit the report to you. Have follow up interviews with employees who continue to make excessive personal telephone calls and start placing written warnings on their files.

Ethnic problems

'One of my employees is constantly making ethnic slurs towards a co-worker. I know I have to step in, but what should I say to her?'

Most work forces (if they're in compliance with the law) are a mixture of individuals of different ethnic backgrounds. Turning the other cheek or tolerating an ethnic slur, whether against a co-worker, a supervisor, a client or someone in the general public, is poor management. An ethnic slur is destructive of the public-good portion of the company image and can undo the efforts put into the human relations among employees.

Jokes at the expense of someone else are not jokes at all. Sometimes the joke-telling gets out of hand and someone's feelings are hurt. Comments of this sort should be discouraged as soon as someone starts *'Did you hear the one about the ...'*

Management should never knowingly joke about someone's background or personal appearance, nor should they condone such behaviour on the part of their employees. One can't judge on the surface how a joke in poor taste might affect an individual. Ethnic comments stem from prejudice - not facts. Prejudice presumes that there's a stereotype of an ethnic group and disregards its members as individuals with different characteristics. Use such reminders as: *'I didn't think that was funny, Paul ...'*

This shows your disapproval and makes the employees more aware that you're monitoring such kinds of jokes. A supervisor's put-down of a slurring joke is indicative of top management's attitude towards any kind of prejudice. Sometimes a private session with the offender is necessary. The supervisor should deal swiftly if the employee insists that the remarks are 'harmless.'

'Tammy, if they're harmless - then they're pointless, so keep your thoughts to yourself.'

If the problem continues, the supervisor should say: *'Tammy, a note is made on each performance appraisal on how employees get along with the other employees (or clients, etc.). I wouldn't like to place a comment on your personnel record that you don't get along, but that's what I'll have to do if you keep making those remarks that I warned you about. Do you understand?'* Or, conduct a formal disciplinary interview explaining the consequences to Tammy if she continues to act as she has in the past.

Buck-Passing Employees

'Maria has a habit of passing-the-buck to other staff members when she's responsible for an error. How can I get her to own up to making mistakes?'

Buck-passing employees can become experts at determining why certain tasks are someone else's responsibility. They say, *'I didn't know I was responsible for that!'* when you'd spent hours explaining the task to them. Others refuse to admit they've made a mistake. They say, *'Who Me? I didn't do that!'* when you both know they were at fault.

Most people take the full blame for their own errors. However, in our more complex managerial environment, it's becoming increasingly important to avoid even minor errors. Buck-passing is often caused by a supervisor's failure to properly delegate responsibility and/or a lack of up-to-date job descriptions. All employees must have a definition of duties set down in the form of a job description manual. Each task should have a performance standard established so that both the employee and the supervisor can monitor how well the employee is doing. This description should be updated regularly (preferably at performance appraisal time).

If not handled correctly, buck-passing can lead to lying, cheating and deep-sixing of mistakes so that no one will find them. The concealment of operating mistakes causes irreparable harm to the company. Service failures can be costly in the short- and long-term dollars. Firstly, there's the cost of the immediate replacement of the service. Secondly, the quality image of the company is impaired so the ultimate sales or services are reduced.

The responsibility definition for each employee is not limited to job training, but should be reinforced from time to time. A typical example might be: *'Maria, you're responsible for correctly matching the freight bills to the duplicate of the receiving report.'*

'What if there are differences?'

'It's part of your duty to note the differences on the voucher to Accounts Payable. Any mistakes in matching will be your fault. Any questions?'

Even if Maria is very suited to the job, she will make mistakes. However, she will make fewer and fewer mistakes and will not attempt to pass the buck on occasion if she's reminded of her responsibility and if she's not over-disciplined for any errors. Over-disciplining may cause such excuses as:

'The dispatcher said it's okay to approve trucking bills - so I thought this was okay too.'

'Don't blame me for that one! John said that it was okay to approve it.'

Setting an example is important. Supervisory personnel will discourage buck-passing by employees if, from time to time (in the presence of their subordinates) they admit to making mistakes themselves. Not every mistake need be admitted to in front of subordinates - however, the admission of an occasional goof on the part of the supervisor will demonstrate to others that passing-the-buck is not desirable.

Work Avoidance

'I have a lazy employee who thinks up many ingenious ways to get out of work. How should I deal with employees who don't do their share of the work or deny making mistakes?'

The first step would to be to check to see that the employee's job description was adequate.

Then have a meeting and discuss what your expectations are.

Disciplining employees can be a problem, whether you manage a business office or supervise a loading dock. Employees use a variety of tactics to avoid work. Being habitually late and being away from their desks are two of the commonest ploys. Deal with these employees by obtaining as much factual information as possible so you can make concrete accusations. Express your concerns over their need to cover-up or deny their mistakes. Explain that you feel it's acceptable for them to make mistakes, but unpardonable for them to try to cover up for those mistakes.

Interrupters

'Sally is constantly interrupting her colleagues with small talk and interferes with the work flow of others.'

This can be a particularly annoying staff member. A certain number of interruptions are part of any job and no one expects workers to refrain from some social exchanges. It's when interruptions get out of hand that action is required. Start by keeping a log to determine how often the person interrupts others, when it happens and for how long. Then explain to Sally what will happen if it continues.

Supervisors may also find that a large portion of their day is spent dealing with their staff's interruptions which are often because they don't rely on their own abilities to make decisions. When an interrupter comes to them with questions, instead of automatically giving the answers to their questions, they should ask the staff member, *'What do you think you should do?'* Their employees usually know what they should be doing, but seek their supervisor's approval anyway. Giving them the chance to learn that they knew the solution before they asked it; is the solution to this annoying habit. Soon, they'll realise that they have the ability to make many more decisions without bothering their supervisor about them.

On the other hand, if supervisors feel that their employees are keeping them from doing your 'real' work - they may need to change their attitude. Perhaps dealing with those so-called interruptions is really an important part of their job - as important as dealing with clients or completing reports. In that case, supervisors need to remind themselves, *'That's my job calling.'* Possibly they're not providing the proper training to help their staff become independent enough to not need their constant approval.

If the above applies to you, try the following:

- Plan short meetings to discuss problems and find solutions to employee concerns.
- Set time limits for meetings and stick to them.
- If your staff is unsure of what to do or their authority level, they may need to have their job descriptions updated.
- Ensure that your staff is adequately trained to do their jobs and give them the authority to handle tasks that really don't need your input or approval.

'The Silent Treatment'

'Jane uses the silent treatment to get her way. If she's upset about something, she clams up and refuses to talk (which can go on for days). What should I do to change her behaviour?'

In modern society, studies show that men and women use the 'silent treatment' equally and both need to be discouraged from using this form of indirect aggression. Ignoring others by refusing to discuss issues is manipulative and unfair and results in a no-win situation for both parties. This isn't to say that people can't walk away from an argument until they calm down, but they must return within a reasonable length of time and resolve the situation with the other person.

Let staff members who use such techniques know that their behaviour is an act of indirect aggression. Explain that they should discuss and resolve annoying situations immediately so they don't accumulate and end up causing a major blow-up later.

When women are asked why they use the silent treatment on men, many reply, *'He never listens to me, so why should I bother to express my opinion?'* This assumption by women comes from differences in male/female communication styles.

Research shows that women face each other directly with eyes anchored on each others' faces when conversing. Men sit at angles to each other and look elsewhere in the room, periodically glancing at each other and often mirror each other's body movements. Men's tendency to face away from women in a conversation, gives women the impression that the men aren't listening. Women also nod their heads much more often than men to show that they're listening and make far more 'listening noises' such as *'um hmmm.'* It's worth taking the effort to explain these differences to both your male and female employees.

Difficult Counselling Interviews

'One of my staff members, Joe, is going through a rough time at home which is drastically affecting his performance at work. It looks as if his marriage is breaking up. How should I approach him to let him know that even though he's going through a rough time, I still need him to do his work?'

'One of my employees, Sandra, is obviously going through a tough time in her personal life. Her elderly mother lives with her and she has to decide whether to put her in a nursing home or not. Her productivity is slipping and she's very withdrawn and doesn't have the same enthusiasm she used to have when dealing with clients. I'd hate to add to her problems, but must see some improvement.'

Personal problems of various kinds can interfere with an employee's performance at work, including:

1. High absentee record;
2. Requests to leave work early;

3. Lateness at the start of work and around coffee and lunch breaks;
4. High number of personal telephone calls;
5. High error rate and breaking of company or safety rules;
6. Little response to group effort;
7. Reduced production;
8. Increased fatigue;
9. Reduced availability for overtime;
10. High 'Sickness' days off;
11. Loss of initiative;
12. Expressions of irritability to co-workers;
13. Requests for irregular vacation time;
14. Antagonism toward supervisor or management;
15. Lower training/learning capability;
16. Low company loyalty; and
17. High grievance rate.

These personal problems may surface that warrant a counselling interview such as:

- family break-up
- alcoholism
- drug abuse
- illness in the home
- problems with children
- problems with spouse

- elderly parents living with them

How should supervisors deal with these problems? Are they qualified to handle them? In most cases - *no* they're not! This is why supervisors should keep abreast of where their staff can go to obtain counselling to solve these kinds of problems. Help them obtain this help - then back off. Make allowances on the job if necessary, but eventually stick to performance issues. Remain objective. Keep emotions in check. It's difficult to think and respond to an employee's need, if you react with emotion yourself.

When dealing with issues of this kind, confidentiality is a must! The employee should be advised that if possible, the matter will go no further than the supervisor. Don't discuss these issues with others unless they're critical to solving the problem. The supervisor can point out the extent to which the employee's performance is below average. Comparisons to previous records can be made. The supervisor can offer assistance in solving the personal problem, but, must stress that suitable performance from the employee must be the end result. For instance:

'I know you're having a bad time right now Joe, but I still need you to keep up our production quotas. Can I count on you to do your share?' Or:

'Sandra, I know that you're capable of better work. Is there some way I can help you to get back on the right track?'

Keep in mind that the problem is the other person's - don't take responsibility for it. Do however try to help him/her get through the problem.

Occasionally counselling interviews can turn out to be difficult ones because of other reasons. A supervisor notices that an employee is snarling at other employees or observes that an employee seems lethargic and their job performance is below normal. The supervisor calls the employee in for a counselling interview. When asked, *'What's the matter?'* the curt reply may be, *'It's none of your business!'*

What would you reply if you were this employee's supervisor? You should say, *'Yes it is. Whenever your behaviour affects your productivity or those around you, it is my business.'* Then encourage him/her to discuss the problem.

If s/he still refuses, add, *'You have two choices. Give me a chance to help you with your problem or get along better with your workmates and improve your job performance (or whatever was the problem). Which have you decided to do?'* Wait for an answer. Then, let him/her know that you expect his/her behaviour to improve and give the consequences should s/he not be willing to change.

What do you say if an employee brings others into the discussion? For instance, *'Joe does that all the time - why are you picking on me?'* Your answer should be, *'We're here to discuss **your** performance - not Joe's.'*

You should then:

- State your perception of the problem and allow the person to think about it.
- State your expectations and keep the door open for further discussions when the employee has cooled down.

This will allow the employee to settle his/her temper and be less emotional or angry when s/he decides to deal with the issue. When you call an employee in to discuss a behaviour or production problem, keep in mind what you wish to accomplish - a change in the employee's behaviour and/or productivity – not retaliation.

Upon becoming aware that the supervisor has noticed a change in attitude or lower performance, the employee may push to solve his/her own problem or at least learn to live with it so it doesn't affect his/her work. The supervisor's duty is to assist a subordinate who has a personal problem, if such assistance is wanted and is possible.

Second, there is the obligation to the company, which requires the best performance possible from each employee. The time to butt into an employee's personal problems is when the supervisor feels s/he can accomplish both these objectives by rendering assistance while maintaining production. A little caution is advisable; *the supervisor should not become directly involved other than as a possible source of advice.*

Sick Leave Abuses

When Bruce entered his office at the beginning of the day he learned that two of his staff had phoned in to say they'd be away from work that day. This seemed to be a regular occurrence and happened far too often. He checked the employee's attendance records and one employee in particular, had been absent more than 21 days that year. This had not been for any lengthy illness, but was scattered with absences of two or three days at a time.

A large contributor to the breakdown of employee morale is the fact that some employees get away with calling in sick, get paid for the day, when they weren't the least bit ill. While it's difficult to determine completely who is truly ill and who isn't, steps can be taken that will likely ensure that the privilege of sick leave with pay is not abused.

Most employees will go to work even with a runny nose and fever and refuse to take advantage of sick pay policies. Many feel that they don't wish to take sick leave for minor ailments because they may need the leave when they're 'really' sick. Others feel that, *'No one can handle my job as well as I can'* and feel some responsibility for their performance. To them, it's part of the ethic of being a good worker. The supervisor should recognise the sacrifices made. When this type of employee calls in sick, s/he is generally too sick to perform any kind of work at all.

Other employees will be out for any and every minor ailment. They view sick leave as a right and want to take full advantage of any accrued leave. They demonstrate little responsibility for their required productivity. The fact that other workers have to carry a larger workload or that their company will suffer economically is of little concern to them.

How many times a year does an employee pull that line before s/he may be considered a chronic absentee? One company says that eight or more absences during a twelve month period indicate a problem employee.

When this type of employee calls and says, *'Sorry boss, but I can't make it in today.'* A seemingly good reply may be: *'Sorry you're ill - stay out until you're feeling better.'* However, don't say that. Don't worry: chronic absentees will stay out until they feel a lot better. Why should they have to knock themselves out? And besides - they view sick leave as their right.

For those suspected of abusing this benefit, the supervisor should call the employee at the end of each work day to ask: *'Orson, how are you coming along? I'm calling to see if you expect to be at work tomorrow.'*

Two beautiful spin-offs benefits can result. First, it has been determined that the absent employee is really at home. (Of course s/he could have been at the doctor's - but *every* time s/he was called?) Second, the employee who becomes aware of the procedure may be discouraged from taking sick leave for seemingly minor ailments or to accomplish some personal chore.

It's generally agreed that innocent absenteeism, even if it is excessive, can't be grounds for disciplinary measures. On the other hand, it's generally agreed that an employee's inability to report for work on a regular basis (for whatever reasons) can be grounds for discharge.

Where the company is faced with the problem of an employee who has been absent from work for excessive periods of time, (i.e. the chronic absentee) s/he may be discharged if the company is able to demonstrate that it's unreasonable for the employment relationship to continue. In such cases:

a. The employer must be able to document the employee's absences, demonstrating not only that they can readily be seen to be well beyond what any reasonable person would

130

consider acceptable, but also that the employee has deviated substantially and unduly from the average level of attendance of other employees;

b. The employer must be able to demonstrate that the excessive absenteeism problem has been persistent and has continued despite <u>documented</u> attempts by the employer to have it corrected. The supervisor must document his/her efforts to counsel the employee and determine underlying reasons for absences. S/he must also be able to show that s/he has had every degree of compassion and has taken into account any 'extenuating circumstances' for excessive absenteeism and has been patient with the employee in attempts to have the problem corrected.

c. The employer must be able to present convincing reasons explaining why s/he feels that there is little or no likelihood of a reduction in the excessive absenteeism in the future. In this regard, the employer is often best advised to provide medical evidence in support of this conclusion.

One employee had been enrolled in a drug rehabilitation program because of abuse of prescription drugs, but still had many days absent from work. The employee always gave a doctor's certificate, but his supervisor wondered how authentic they were. How could he make sure that his staff's absences were because they were legitimately sick and not taking the day off because of other reasons or had slipped in their rehabilitation program?

Many employees abuse a company's sick leave by using sick leave for one of the following reasons:

- their children are sick;
- their spouse is sick;
- they just wanted a day off;
- for 'personal reasons' (too varied to list); or
- had abused drugs or alcohol.

Should a supervisor pay his or her staff when they're away for these kinds of absences? It depends on the supervisor and their office policy and award agreement. Unless covered by an award, sick leave is given to employees for their own illness, not for the sickness of someone else or for other reasons. Other companies provide additional paid leave such as compassionate leave (for critical illness or death in the family) or jury duty leave. Still others allow a set number of days for family emergencies or sickness. This is often put into a broad category entitled 'general or personal leave.' This can be used for family or personal emergencies, but again employees are cautioned not to abuse the privilege. They must require the day off because of a legitimate emergency.

So what can a supervisor do if s/he feels employees are abusing their paid time off privileges? Usually a simple reminder about the abuse of the sick leave policy will stop the abuse. If the absences become chronic, it's generally agreed that an employee's inability to report for work on a regular basis (for whatever reasons) can be grounds for termination.

In industries where there is a heavier reliance on individual performance and any absence is a disruption in the flow of service to customers, management has to rely more on stiffer illness verification procedures including the following:

1. Required doctor's certificate for three or more consecutive sick days.
2. Doctor's certificate for any absence due to illness before or after a holiday weekend.

3. Complete physical examination by the company doctor if the employee is out more than ten days in any one year.

What should the supervisor do, when forced to question a doctor's certificate verifying the employee's illness? S/he should investigate. When an employee is found guilty of falsifying a doctor's certificate, s/he can and should be disciplined. The degree of discipline depends on the circumstances of the particular case.

The Alcoholic Employee

'One of my staff - Charlie - has come back from lunch under the influence of alcohol. I have sent him home when this occurs, but it's become a regular thing with him. He's been away several days around the weekend, which I suspect have been because he was drinking and had to sober up. How am I to deal with an employee who appears to have become an alcoholic?'

Experienced supervisors will advise that any promise by an employee that s/he can control his/her alcoholic habit must be viewed with suspicion. S/he would not admit to him/herself (much less to the boss) that s/he has a drinking problem. This makes for a strong distinction between the alcoholic and the other types of problem employees who frequently admit to their shortcomings.

Most people drink and even though some may be considered heavy drinkers, not all become alcoholics. The few that do can be helped more successfully if help is offered in the early stages. Generally the drinker who has become an alcoholic will begin to incur a heavy absentee record - not necessarily typified by the Monday and Friday syndrome. (Frequently s/he has dried out by Monday and if Friday is payday s/he needs the cash). Partial attendance can be expected.

Either related illness forces him/her to be late or s/he leaves after lunch break. Sometimes food has made the employee ill or s/he may wish to indulge the weakness.

When questioned about the absences or the partial absences, the alcoholic can't be expected to admit to the real cause, but will offer any excuse. Supervisors must realise that this kind of problem is beyond his/her realm of responsibility. Employees with this problem must be encouraged to obtain help from their family doctor, Alcoholics Anonymous or any other source available to him/her. The supervisor must, however, be very firm in stating to the employee that failures in performance must be corrected and it's up to the employee to find a way to accomplish this.

When an employee's problem of excessive absenteeism is due to drug or alcohol abuse, the employer may discharge the employee if s/he is able to demonstrate that the 'employment relationship' cannot reasonably be reconstructed. In such cases, the employer must be able to define that decision in relation to the type of criteria noted above. As well however, the employer must show that s/he has recognised the alcoholic problem as an illness and has made every effort to assist the employee in efforts to correct the illness. Any rehabilitation efforts will be carefully reviewed and the company must be convinced that further efforts at rehabilitation are not likely to be successful.

A frequent attribute of the problem of the alcoholic employee is that many co-workers and supervisors wish to conceal the problem. They have a desire to 'help' the employee by not permitting the higher levels of management to be aware that one of their employees is an alcoholic. For some reason, this type of cover-up is not tried with other types of problems, but genuinely peculiar to employee alcoholism (and drug abuse). Some of the reasons used for covering up for the alcoholic include:

1. Charlie's a good worker.
2. He needs the job and getting caught would sink his ship.
3. He has a lot of problems at home.
4. He would help anybody he could.
5. It's an illness that can't be cured by letting management know.
6. It will only take a short while to sober him up.
7. The job caused him to drink.

In circumstances such as these, the employee may run circles around his/her supervisors and co-workers who mistakenly believe they can help the employee by covering up his/her actions. One way of overcoming the willingness to conceal the alcoholic employee is to set the record straight with regard to all alcoholics:

1. If the alcoholic employee drives to and from work or uses a company vehicle, s/he may be a deadly menace to him/herself as well as to others on the road.

2. The alcoholic is a threat to his/her own safety and that of others while on the job. *If an alcoholic injures him/herself at work while intoxicated, s/he generally cannot obtain worker's compensation for any job-related injury.* Also: *Other injured employees may not recover worker's compensation and may have to lodge a personal law suit against the alcoholic to pay for any time off because of an injury.*

3. An alcoholic doesn't get cured by someone's covering up for him/her. S/he continues to be a problem both at work and at home.

4. The company's community relations suffer if other organised groups in the community see in the company image, a tolerance for alcoholism.

5. If an employee has customer contact while intoxicated, s/he will cause a loss of sales and company image.

6. Many employees, clients and parents of some of the younger employees, are offended by the presence of an alcoholic employee on the premises.

7. An alcoholic can only be cured with the assistance of experienced persons who are skilled in such matters.

8. An alcoholic employee, besides problems with tardiness and absenteeism, may:

o   Disregard safety rules;
o   Be indifferent to productivity requirements;
o   Have a higher error rate;
o   Drink on the premises;
o   Steal company and/or other employee's property; and
o   Encourage others to violate company rules.

Managerial and other personnel will do well to advise the alcoholic employee that drinking is a problem that s/he hasn't been able to handle on his/her own; that they understand that s/he has a problem and will do what they can to help. While only s/he can stop the drinking, the associates should applaud the alcoholic's effort to overcome the problem.

Supervisors and other management personnel should be made aware that cover-up of the existence of alcoholic employees will not be tolerated and that the company has rules regarding the handling of employees who drink on the job. If an employee is interested in helping the alcoholic, there are ways - not by trying to cover up for him/her, but by encouraging him/her to seek assistance.

Messy work area

'Darren is a very messy person and his work area is a disaster waiting to happen. How can I get him to tidy up his work area?'

This is a necessity under work cover regulations. Many think that having a messy work station is not a requirement of the job. They consider it window dressing, for they believe that an operation can be just as productive no matter what the housekeeping conditions are. However, some of the characteristics that do affect efficiency and are evidence of poor housekeeping include:

1. Missing records or files.
2. Lost or misplaced tools or equipment.
3. High supply costs.
4. Improper mix of parts and inventory.
5. High contamination of product.
6. High scrap and rework costs.
7. Poor balance of finished products inventory.
8. High machine down-time.
9. Poor safety record.
10. Low employee morale;

11. Disinterest in working overtime.
12. Discipline problems and labour turnover.

One way to motivate the employees to maintain a tidy work area is to set an example. If the supervisor's office is neat and clean, then good housekeeping habits are more easily encouraged among the rank and file. Encourage daily clean up at the end of the day. If the supervisor spots someone whose workstation looks messy heading for the door, s/he should stop the employee and ask him/her to organise his/her workstation before leaving. For more difficult problems, a written checklist of housekeeping activities could be given to messy employees.

Sloppy or Careless

'One of my staff completes her work so poorly, that someone else has to re-do her effort. This often takes more time than the original task. I'd hate to have to fire her, but unless her productivity improves I'm afraid that's what I'll have to do.'

Have you been clear to her what you expect from her? Is her job description adequate? Does it outline the tasks she must do and have standards of performance or benchmarks that she's expected to reach when performing those tasks? If not - the fault could be yours.

Or it's possible that she has been in a 'rut' for so long that it will take considerable effort for her to 'dig herself out.' Unfortunately, she possibly doesn't perceive that she's in a rut and plods along, day after day, year after year, often performing tasks she can barely tolerate doing. Her entire life may be routine and mundane and she may not have considered there are other options open to her.

Short of putting a bomb under her, there's not much you can do to get her motivated. Motivation has to come from within herself, but start by letting her know what is expected of her. Then be ready to initiate the disciplinary process outlining the consequences she will face if she does not improve her performance.

The Bottleneck Employee

'The work isn't getting out because George isn't doing his part!'

Bottlenecks are a frequent management complaint. The causes could be attributable to either the management's design of the work flow or to an employee's poor work habits.

Management's poor design of the work flow can be detected by a simple test. Have another employee assume the duties of the employee in the problem area. If there's still a bottleneck (after the training period) then changes may have to be made to the work flow arrangements.

Here are the typical characteristics of a bottleneck employee:

1. They have poor time management skills.
2. Too many items are held up because of relatively minor problems.
3. Have not had enough training.
4. Have low decision-making capability.
5. Are unaware of supervisor's expectations.
6. Square peg in round hole - qualifications don't fit requirements of the job or they lack teamwork skills.
7. Feel threatened by job insecurity.
8. Have an unusual fear of making mistakes. Or,
9. Involved in personality clashes with supervisors or colleagues resulting in a lack of cooperation between staff.

Where there's no indication that the employee is being a deliberate bottleneck, some additional on-the-job training may be in order to ensure employee understands what the job entails. During this re-training, the supervisor can see if the employee understands his/her job responsibilities. S/he can demonstrate to the employee how to perform the various tasks and then guide him/her under direct observation. Little techniques that speed the job along should be emphasised.

If employees are more aware of what functions are performed before or after theirs, they can use their judgement and understand the consequences of their own performance. Employees will learn how their jobs fit into the total picture and what contribution they're expected to make.

Most 'sticks-in-the-mid' don't really want to be 'sticks-in-the mud.' Nearly everyone wants to feel that s/he is co-operating to achieve common goals. The ploy is to make everyone in the work force have a common goal. Other employees can be encouraged to assist:

'Tom, can you show Rick how he can move that project faster?'

'Rick, let Tom show you a couple of techniques for pushing the stuff through that we need now.'

Encourage the problem employee to want to put the work out faster. The paying of a few compliments here and there improves confidence among slower employees. It permits them to have a greater feeling of job security and certainly reduces tensions. The bottleneck employee can become less fearful of incidental mistakes, thus reducing his/her own built-in need for more control of his/her work.

Error-Prone Employees

'Phil is our departmental disaster who makes so many mistakes I often wonder if he isn't doing so on purpose to evade doing his job. He's an intelligent man, but still makes the most unusual mistakes. How can I turn him around and improve his accuracy rate?'

Just as auto insurance companies recognise that some drivers are more prone to having accidents than the general population of drivers, some recognition must be given to the fact that some employees are more likely to make mistakes than others. Of course, deliberate mistakes are a cause for the use of disciplinary measures up to and including firing the errant employee. However, most mistakes are not intentional. They are caused by a variety of reasons, including errors of judgement on the part of management.

There are two basic kinds of mistakes; system mistakes and human mistakes. The first results from the design of a system. Constant improvement of the system will reduce the error rate.

No matter how well the system is designed, there is a certain amount of reliance on the human factor. That factor is the one to which line management personnel have to apply a great deal of attention. The system's designer may also be at fault of the 'human' mistakes. Some of the following conditions may also exist:

1. Inadequate job training.
2. Limited written instructions.
3. Large number of subordinates reporting to one supervisor (12 should be the maximum number of subordinates reporting to one supervisor).
4. Too few intermediate levels of supervision.
5. Dull working environment.
6. Job boredom.
7. Poor analysis of error cause.
8. High employee turnover.

Most employees like to feel that they're earning their pay. Part of that feeling of pride stems from their opinion that their work has few if any errors. Therefore, they appreciate help - when offered gracefully - to improve their own pride in their work. One method of attack is to provide an employee-coach for the error-prone employee. A senior employee, who is proficient in his/her job, will be able to isolate the causes of the problem employee's errors and provide instruction in special techniques to either avoid such errors or catch the mistakes and take corrective action. To minimise carelessness, the problem employee has to be shown at which points in the process, some additional attention should be applied:

'Arnold, could you spend a little more time rechecking your work?'

'Donna, can you pay a little more attention to these types of items?'

Employee Daydreaming

'Mary has just announced that she's engaged to be married. This is great – but she spends too much of her time thinking and daydreaming about her wedding and is so

distracted that her work is suffering. How can I get her back on track?'

We all daydream, but some people do it to excess - to a point where it interferes with work or productivity or becomes a dangerous safety problem. In this case Mary is distracted because of her wedding. Speak to her and let her know that her productivity is down and that you're counting on her to give the same work as she did before the announcement of her wedding. She must know you're serious and will have no choice but to start formal disciplinary matters if her productivity doesn't improve.

Some jobs lend themselves more to employee daydreaming than others and have to be monitored more carefully. It's not always fair to pin the blame for daydreaming on the employee. His/her job may be so boring the employee can't keep his/her mind on it. Machine-like functions tend to create opportunities for daydreaming. Where greater worker attention is required, daydreaming can result in loss of productivity, errors and even accidents. The problem may be that the job was not designed to hold the employee's attention.

The design of the work area can reduce the tendency to daydream. Operations that must be performed while standing, tend to discourage day-dreaming. The work area decor is of some importance. Desks or work areas need not be all the same colour. Attempts should be made to eliminate monotony in the work environment. This is why job rotation is so popular.

Those work situations that require a higher degree of creativity on the part of the employee should have an environment that's conducive to creativity. If there's any flexibility in the method of performing the task, add that flexibility to the task description. This will allow the employee to decide how to handle particular steps by using his/her initiative in selecting his/her production process. Such flexibility permits the employee to think about how s/he wants to handle a particular job and therefore increases his/her alertness and reduces monotony.

No matter what efforts are made to dispel daydreaming potential, some employees seem to be lost in the clouds. Only constant supervisory attention can dispel the problem and keep the employee on his/her toes.

Sometimes, a discussion between the supervisor and the employee is in order.

Show-offs

'I have an employee who is a real show-off and at our training sessions, he's the class clown. His actions interfere with the smooth-running of our department and training sessions are almost a waste of time because of his antics.'

Show-offs must be the centre of attention. They play games on others - interrupt them with childish antics. They can have the 'class clown' mentality where they seek others' attention by fooling around. Getting them to accomplish tasks can be a heavy chore. They accomplish this by escalating the value of what they do, where they've been and whom they know. They exaggerate their own importance to win admiration or attention and have the habit of snubbing people they don't think of as important. They're snooty and snobbishly superior. Being high achievers, they put themselves high on their own list of priorities.

Make sure he doesn't take an unfair share of credit for assignments done in a team environment. He needs praise, so give praise where praise is deserved and correct him when he tries to exaggerate his contributions. If he acts up at meetings - take him aside. Use feedback to explain what his behaviour does to others and the hardships it causes to his other team members. A clearly defined job description about how he is to complete tasks is a must. If his behaviour continues - begin disciplinary steps with written warnings.

Won't answer phone calls and emails

'Two of my staff are terrible communicators. One doesn't return phone calls - the other doesn't answer e-mails.'

The possibility is that you might be communicating to them using an incorrect 'sensory language.'

When we say two people have 'rapport,' we usually mean that their relationship is harmonious - we get into someone else's world. We can enhance this rapport by determining another's primary sensory language. Most of us are a mixture of all three, but one usually stands out as being our primary sensory language.

People process information in different ways. They are primarily visual, auditory or kinaesthetic (muscular movement) in the way they process information. Each type uses distinctive words that reflect their preference. To create rapport with people, listen to find their primary mode of communication then mirror their language. Here are examples of these:

The visual person might say:

'I get the picture.'
'I see what you mean.'
'Let me see what the job looks like.' or,
'My perception is....'

The auditory person uses such phrases as:
'That sounds good to me.'
'I hear what you're saying.'
'That rings a bell.'
'I hear you loud and clear.' or,
'Let me explain how this works.'

Typical phrases for kinaesthetic would be:
'Show me how to do this.'
'That doesn't feel right.'
'Hold on.'
'I'm comfortable with that.'
'That's a rough problem.' or,
'You have a heavy task.'

Is it possible that the one who doesn't answer his/her phone calls is a visual person and the one who doesn't answer his/her emails is an auditory one? Just changing your method of communication might be the answer to these problems.

CHAPTER 3

DIFFICULT SITUATIONS
- COLLEAGUES & OTHERS

Answering Phone Messages

'I'm a receptionist and find that some people don't return their phone messages. Mr. Bailey had tried five times to reach Mr. Smith and I placed the messages on his desk throughout the day. I know Mr. Smith wasn't very busy that day and had ample time to answer the messages. The fifth time Mr. Bailey called; he accused me of not passing on his messages. I've had enough of this person's poor business practices, but don't know how to approach him about the problem.'

Most companies these days have voice mail. Why has your company not installed this device? However, this doesn't answer your request. Use the following technique whenever anyone is making your life miserable - whether it is someone who isn't returning phone calls or doesn't have his or her information ready for your department's monthly reports.

Say, *'I have a problem and I need your help in solving it.'* Then discuss the problem. *'Mr.*

155

Bailey called and left messages for you five times today. I placed those messages on your desk. The last time he phoned, he accused me of not passing your messages on to you. What should I tell him the next time he calls?' This way, you dump the problem on the lap of the person who caused it and most feel obliged to help you solve the problem. It's far better to use this tactic than saying, *'You turkey – why don't you answer your phone calls?'*

Dysfunctional childhood

'My co-worker, Bill, grew up in a dysfunctional environment. He was beaten and yelled at most of his life and suffered from a barrage of constant put-downs. Repeatedly, he was told he was 'stupid, dumb and wouldn't amount to anything.' He firmly believes that his future won't be any different from his past so resists making decision that will alter his life. How can I make him see that his future is what he makes of it and his past is not a blueprint for his life hereafter?'

Many people spend their lives reliving the past. They get into a mental rut that concentrates on what was, rather than what will be. Many of their comments start with the prefaces, *'I should have ...'* Or, *'If only I had ...'*

156

When people drift through life, rather than controlling it, I think of them as 'stuck.' They'll remain stuck where they are, unless *they* do something to change their lives. They waste their lives by getting in a rut and staying there or making feeble stabs at changing their lives. The least kind of opposition sends them scuttling back towards their safety net of sameness. These people hate getting up in the morning, because there's not much that's exciting or stimulating in their lives. One day is just like another and the future's likely to be the same. These people need a jolt to get them living again. Just as heart-attack victims need a jolt of electricity to get their hearts restarted; these people need a jolt of reality to put them back into the land of the living.

Let's put ourselves into Bill's shoes for a while and feel what he might be feeling:

He accepts criticism as always being true. Not only does he accept criticism from others willingly, he's the one who criticises everything he does himself as well. The little voice in his head is always ridiculing him about his perceived failures. He punishes himself with statements such as *'I'm too old ... I'm not smart enough ... I'm not good at that.'*

What he's stating is, *'I'm a finished product in this area and I'm never going to be different.'*

His fear of failure is very often the fear of someone else's disapproval or ridicule. Failure is someone else's opinion of how certain acts should be completed, so he doesn't attempt anything new or challenging. He'll shun experiences that might bring failure and avoids anything that doesn't guarantee success. He may turn down excellent opportunities, but can't explain why he's doing so.

He hasn't learned how to be assertive - to stand up for himself. Inexperienced in the art of getting his own needs met, he allows others to manipulate him. He's unable to make decisions that support his own wishes, values and feelings. The result is that he feels bad about himself without knowing why.

He constantly compares himself to others. Others are always happier, more famous, more successful or worth more. Others' successes only make him more depressed at his own status in life. He may feel that if he fails at something, that he's a failure as a person. Instead of trying another avenue or another way of doing something, he quits trying.

Using 20/20 hindsight, he can probably see exactly where he went wrong - on a job interview or in a love relationship. These thoughts can cause immobility and make him remain in the negative rut he's in.

So how do you help this kind of individual? Encourage him to stop thinking of life in black or white terms. There are many grey areas in between. Deal with him by having a heart-to-heart talk with him. Identify his negative behaviour and ask his permission to bring this behaviour to his attention if you hear him running himself down or reliving his past. Once a person is an adult, there's no excuse to blame a terrible childhood or a failure at school for what's going to happen in their future. He must change his attitude about this to become 'unstuck.'

If life doesn't come up to his expectations, console him with the idea that it's never too late for conditions to change. Instead of dwelling in the past, he needs to concentrate his energy on building a better, happier life and make the most of the present moment.

He can't acquire the trait of extending himself to the utmost overnight. Confidence is a cumulative feeling. There will likely be setbacks and disappointments, but:

Someone who tries to do something and fails is a lot better off than the person who tries to do nothing and succeeds.

Encourage Bill to get professional counselling to counteract his dysfunctional childhood and introduce him to good role models. Your moral support will make this transition considerably easier for him.

Serviceman gets uncivil treatment

'I'm a serviceman for business machines and find myself becoming angrier and angrier by the attitude of the people I've come to help. I'm blamed because the machine has broken down, but they often don't stay around to explain the exact problem they're facing. This means I have to check out the entire machine that costs the companies much more. My second beef is that I'm treated as if I'm a non-person or as if I'm part of the machine. It's no wonder that service people don't last long in my business!'

We all need to look at how we treat people who work in the service industry. Ask yourself whether you commit the following actions that are degrading and can have devastating effects on others:

1. Do you release your frustrations about the broken business machine on the service representative? *'It's about time you got here. This machine hasn't been working properly all day!'*
2. Do you fail to recognise service people by treating them as if they weren't there?
3. Do you fail to keep them informed about problems you're facing or have faced in the past?
4. Do you forget to thank them for fixing your problem?

If you're guilty of the above actions, try a little empathy and realise that the service representatives are doing their best to keep your machines in working order. If you're the service representative, say, *'I'm doing my best to help you, but you're not making it very easy for me to do so. I need to ask you some questions, so I can hone in on the problems you're facing. Then I can fix your machine and allow you to get on with your work.'* This should at least get some of the help you need to get the job done.

'My problem is that clients come on to me and make passes when I make service calls. How can I deal with this without offending the client?'

This is a problem faced by both men and women when they enter the domain or 'home turf' of clients. Be as businesslike as possible when visiting clients. If the client shows signs of being amorous, (such as suggesting that you get together for lunch) explain that you'd rather not mix your business with your personal life - and stick to it.

If they persist and become aggressive in their advances, more drastic actions are required. Say, *'Your actions are upsetting me. I've told you twice that I'm not interested in pursuing a personal relationship with you. If you continue to talk and act in this manner, I'll have no other recourse but to charge you with sexual harassment.'*

In the latter case, you would document the incident. Tell your supervisor that you were forced to threaten the client with sexual harassment charges and give him or her, a copy of your documentation. If your supervisor is enlightened, s/he will follow-up with a verbal or written confirmation to the client about your treatment and reinforce your actions. If I were your supervisor, I'd also talk to the client's superiors and make them aware of the problems the employee is causing to the staff member. It's likely that this client treats other people in a similar fashion and their employer will likely want to take steps to stop his/her behaviour before the situation ends up in a court battle.

Customer Service

'One of my colleagues embarrasses me by the way he treats customers. He's rude, gives poor service and generally makes our department look bad.'

Customers are no different from anyone else in that they appreciate courtesy. One thing a salesperson must never forget is that the customer is number one. Sadly, some salespeople give the impression that looking after the customer is an interruption to their 'real work.' Such behaviour implies that the salesperson is doing clients a favour by helping them. In reality, the customer's needs should take precedence over any other work they do.

Customer service of course, is not just important for those who work in stores and restaurants. Every kind of organisation that exists in society needs proper customer service. Rudeness, impatience and insensitivity are not compatible with good, professional sales. Even so, salespeople sometimes display these negative traits. Discourtesy, disrespect, indifference, slow service, ignorance of the services offered by the company, errors and negative behaviour repel customers and leave bad feelings. Customers often respond to the bad feelings by simply staying away.

Customers gravitate to places where they get the most positive feelings. The way salespeople act with customers is far more important than all the company money spent on advertising and image building. The most successful members of service organisations share common traits. They learn everything they possibly can about their organisation and how it can serve its clients better.

Knowledgeable salespeople know:

- What their organisation does.
- Who their key personnel are.
- Why the organisation works the way it does.
- What services or products it offers.

- What common questions or problems are likely to arise
- How they can help clients more effectively.

Show your colleague where you think he's falling down in his service to the customers using feedback to explain how you feel when he does this. It just takes one inefficient salesperson to destroy what has taken your company years to build and you don't want to be part of the problem by ignoring his poor service. If he refuses to change, document the bad service he has given and explain your concerns to your supervisor.

Colleague has tantrums

'Sue, one of my colleagues has tantrums. You've told us how to deal with bosses who have tantrums - but how do you deal with colleagues?'

Keep in mind that someone who is having a tantrum is not acting reasonably. Anyone who is not acting reasonably is temporarily insane. If you yell back at them - all you have is two people having an insane conversation. Your goal when coping with a person having a tantrum is to help them re-gain control. So:

1. Keep your cool and be firm. Make it clear that you intend to cool down the situation before continuing your discussion.
2. If Sue won't calm down, ask her what she would call such behaviour if one of her children acted the same way. Threaten to walk away from her if she won't calm down. Follow-through if she continues.
3. If she does calm down, ask for facts about the situation.
4. Listen carefully and then do what you can to resolve the dispute.
5. She may regret her outburst. Be ready to deal with her guilt feelings.

Obviously, she doesn't know how to handle anger; otherwise she wouldn't allow herself to get to this stage. Most tantrum givers have feelings of fear, helplessness and frustration. They have low self-esteem and many take every affront personally. As a child they likely found that tantrums allowed them to get their way - so why stop doing something that's so effective? This disruptive behaviour often continues into adulthood, but at that stage of their lives, their tantrums produce a greater backlash of anger and resistance than any of the other difficult behaviours.

If the situation is repetitive and on-going, it's likely that this person has tantrums in front of others as well. So ask for others' help in stopping this unacceptable behaviour.

What a chauvinist!

'He did it again! He made another chauvinistic remark! He insists on calling me 'his girl.' Well I haven't been a 'girl' since I was twelve! Where has he been for the past twenty years? I'm so tired of chauvinistic men!'

Bill, a senior officer in her organisation had embarrassed her again at the last manager's meeting. She had made a minor mistake on a report. He patted her on the head and said, *'It's okay. You're very smart for a woman.'* She was so shocked that she couldn't reply.

Chauvinism is behaviour displayed by both men and women who believe that the world should be male dominated and that men are superior to women. This can still be a serious problem for women in the work place.

There are two forms of male chauvinism. The first kind is blatant. The woman *knows* this man is out to make women feel bad, to put them down and to keep them in their 'place.' They may refer to a woman in a management position as their 'token woman.' Women should stick to the facts when dealing with this kind of individual. If a man says, *'You're earning a good salary for a woman.'*

The woman should reply, *'You believe that women should earn less than men?'*

He says, *'Yes, I do.'*

She says, *'I hear what you're saying. I believe women deserve an equal chance to earn the same kind of salary as men. Women pay rent like men, pay the same for food as men and definitely pay taxes like men. What are the reasons for your belief that women should earn less than men?'* This starts a dialogue instead of ending up in a confrontation.

Why do some men feel the need to use this intentional type of chauvinism? They use it to put women down, which in turn makes *them* feel more important. So how should a woman respond to intentional chauvinism? A calm, *'That was a very chauvinistic remark you just made. What did you really mean by that comment?'* Or, *'That was a very sarcastic and hurting remark you just made. Can you explain why you felt the need to make such a comment?'*

Another tactic is, instead of reacting to the chauvinistic remark, tune it out and ignore it. By remaining calm the victim maintains control. The true chauvinist can't handle this behaviour, because the woman isn't drawn into playing the game. It's no fun any more - so they take their chauvinistic remarks elsewhere.

The other form of chauvinism is more subtle and is used by men who often aren't aware that their actions could be classified as chauvinistic. These are usually older men, who are sixty years of age or older or men whose upbringing or home situation conditioned them to believe that they are to protect and care for women. Many of these men call women 'dear' because women *are* dear to them.

Because these men don't use this type of chauvinism to hurt women, a gentle response from women is advisable. They often don't know that what they do or say may be offensive to women. Unless the women let them know there's a problem, they're not going to change, so it's up to women to speak up. *'I don't know if you're aware of this or not, but many women would find your last comment to be chauvinistic or patronising. I'm not*

169

offended by your calling me 'Dear,' but other women might be.'

If a woman is promoted into a senior position and finds she is the only female at that level, she may suffer from isolation. The male managers have coffee and lunch together and may not think to include her in their plans. This leaves her with the choice of having breaks with her female support staff or finding other senior women in her company (or others) for socialising.

Sarcasm

'Will I never learn? Why did I let him goad me into getting mad again?'

Paul, a co-worker was the most sarcastic person she knew. He threw his barbs at Sandra relentlessly. Their last exchange went as follows:

Paul: *'Give women an inch and they'll take a mile. Pretty soon we won't have any say in what's happening in the world.'*

Sandra retaliated with: *'Well, with 52 per cent of the population being women and only 48 per cent men, what do you expect - the same paternalistic society we've suffered through for centuries?'*

Who was in control of this sarcastic exchange? Sandra, the recipient of the sarcasm is - until she replies. Did Sandra respond correctly by using sarcasm herself? No - she relinquished the control, which will likely not stop Paul's barrage. Sandra could have stopped the sarcasm by sticking to facts and determining what Paul was trying to tell her. If she'd done this, the following conversation would occur:

Paul: *'Give women an inch and they'll take a mile. Pretty soon we won't have any say in what's happening in the world.'*

Sandra: *'What's happening that you object to?'*

Paul: *'Women want too many extras in the work place.'*

Sandra: *'What extras?'*

Paul: *'Day care, for instance. Why is it necessary? Too many women work. They should be at home with their families.'*

Sandra: *'How many women do you think work because they have to?'*

Paul: *'Not many.'*

Sandra: *'Over three-quarters have to work because their families can't survive without both incomes. Over half of working women are the sole breadwinners for themselves and their children. These children need adequate day-care. It's not a frill, but a necessity for most women. Do you feel women should be shouldering the full responsibility or should the men be taking part in this?'*

You can see that Sandra is combating the sarcasm with facts, not emotions and keeps Paul on topic. As the conversation progresses, he uses less and less sarcasm and they end up in a discussion rather than a debate.

There are two basic kinds of sarcasm. Some sarcasm is nothing more than harmless kidding that's humorous for all concerned. Many comedians use it, as do good friends. It's non-threatening because the speakers make fun of themselves or situations. They do not use it to put others down. Strong laughter at a joke can relieve headaches and lower a person's blood pressure and create bonds between people. The urge to share a joke of this kind is almost irresistible.

The second kind is hurtful and designed to make others feel small - the kind Paul used on Sandra. This type of sarcasm occurs because it's no longer acceptable to hit others with fists, so cutting words (sarcasm) is used instead. It's a form of indirect aggression; one of the most manipulative methods of getting one's way. Those using it feel a sense of power at seeing other people squirm, pointing out and laughing at others' shortcomings.

Because their jest is often subtle and open to more than one interpretation, it can be used to communicate taboo interests and values, to probe for what the other person is thinking or to make a suggestion the joker is not sure will be accepted. Through their joking comments, they can mention forbidden subjects, engage in offensive or childish behaviour and even step out of the bounds of good taste.

It's important that we look behind the reasons people use the hurting, cutting kind of sarcasm. It's because it makes **them** feel more important. Emotionally, they don't feel very good about themselves, so they put others down to make themselves feel more important. The game continues when others respond defensively or act hurt. They're happiest when others get angry and defend themselves.

These people resort to the hurting kind of sarcasm to express negative emotions. They're usually reluctant to confront the cause of their sarcastic remarks directly. They accomplish this through pranks, ridicule or jokes at someone else's expense. Examples of conversations using hurting sarcasm are:

'You finally decided to honour us with your presence.'

'That outfit looks like it came off the ark.'

'Ray did such a good job on his last project that the company demoted him.'

'If you're so smart, why aren't you my supervisor?'

'You're not exactly Mr. Efficiency yourself/'

'Mark's so smart - he got forty per cent on his last marketing exam.'

You've just tipped over a cup of coffee. Comment, *'You didn't miss any of us with your coffee this time did you?'*

You ask a person to repeat a comment. They reply, *'Is English your second language?'*

Instead of reacting to his sarcasm - she should turn it off. If she can't stay quiet, has tried logic and feels his actions warrant an answer, she could try, *'Your last comment was very sarcastic and a put-down. Put-downs hurt. Can you explain why you said what you did?'* Or, *'Why did you feel you had to give me a put down like that?'*

Another approach to sarcasm is to say, *'That was pretty sarcastic. What did you really mean to say that you're covering up with sarcasm?'* This should at least cause him to analyse why he made the remark and what he really meant to accomplish with his remarks. This makes him account for his actions. He might not be aware of how destructive his behaviour is to others.

Use the following comments *only* if you don't want the person to speak to you again say, *'Your last comment was very sarcastic and a put down. What is it about me that makes you feel so intimidated, that you use such cutting sarcastic remarks?'*

Sarcasm can also be a defensive move and Paul may have felt the need to defend himself. Could Sandra have put Paul on the defensive with her actions or could he perceive that she was responsible for a putdown he received? Was she better looking, did the vice-president of the company like her better or did she get the promotion he wanted? When she understands the hidden motives behind his sarcasm she should be able to handle it better.

She also needs to be aware that men and women use sarcasm differently. For instance, men are often very sensitive about baldness, so, when a man's buddies notice a small bald patch on his head, he'll likely receive a new nick-name, 'Baldy.' Could you imagine what would happen if women did this to each other? For instance, can you really picture one woman saying to another, *'How are you doing today, flabby thighs?'* It's likely that the other woman would never speak to her again!

Unless women grow up with brothers who use this form of sarcasm, they react as if the man has hit them. In a way he has - verbally, so many act hurt and become defensive. The man's reaction to her behaviour is often, *'Can't you take a joke?'* Women should ask the giver of the sarcasm to explain the 'joke' to them.

Power Trips

'One woman at work is power-hungry. Even though Jennifer has a junior role, she tries to lord it over her co-workers and makes us know that she expects to be our supervisor soon. Why does she do this and how can we deal with her awful attitude problem?'

Power is influence over other people or can just be not being dependent on others. Those who are overcome with their own power stay preoccupied with their own needs and are often oblivious to the wishes and desires of less powerful people. They must be in charge of every transaction whether they have the authority to do so or not.

Should Julie be placed into a supervisory position, she would have trouble adjusting to how she should act and misunderstand her role. She's obviously observed other manipulative managers who misused their power by their domineering, intimidating and even bullying behaviour. She needs to understand that her present display of strength and power is probably due to and used to cover up for how inadequate she feels.

Co-operation is the name of the game and gives a person true power and influence over others. Only when trust is established will people want to follow the person's lead. You cannot buy respect, but she seems to think she can do so by her constant need to be in charge.

Leadership can be demonstrated with a simple piece of string. Pull it and it will follow wherever you wish. Push it and it will go nowhere at all. If people don't follow a supervisor's lead voluntarily - if they always have to be forced - that person's not a good leader.

When socialising, this kind of person is the one who treats service people like dirt. She does everything she can, to make their jobs difficult, yet complains if the person retaliates with less than his/her best service.

At present, she may not even be aware that she is antagonising others. Don't let this tyrant continue to use this behaviour in your presence. It's up to you to bring this offending habit to her attention. If she tries to lord it over you at work - let her know that you don't appreciate her behaviour. If she belittles service staff - do the same.

PROCESS OF FEEDBACK

1. Describe the problem or situation to the person causing the difficulty. Give examples.
2. Define what feelings or reactions his/her behaviour causes you (sadness, anger, anxiety, hurt or upset).

3. Suggest a solution or ask them to provide one.

The problem: *'Last week you belittled both me and other service staff in public. You don't have the right to do this.'*

Your feelings or reactions: *'I found this very patronising and embarrassing for everyone.'*

The solution: *'In the future I won't put up with such behaviour and will challenge your right to use such manipulative tactics.'*

What she does about it is her business, but at least she will know that you won't tolerate that behaviour any more. If all her co-workers use this tactic, she will soon stop the behaviour because she'll realise that all she's doing is making enemies. The supervisor should have stepped in and dealt with the problem.

Problem Meeting Participants

'I hate our weekly meetings! We never accomplish anything and we waste so much time and people walk in late. And those who come to the meetings aren't much help either with the bickering, procrastinating and promising they'll do something when everyone else knows they'll renege as usual.'

Meetings are notorious for wasting time. Many shouldn't be held and others could use conference phone calls to settle issues instead of people having to fly from far off branches to attend meetings. Do suggest alternatives to those who hold these unnecessary meetings. Be sure to outline the advantages and disadvantages of having the meetings at such set times and those for having meetings only when they're necessary. Here are some guidelines on how to deal with the bickering, procrastinating and people who promise but don't follow-through:

Dealing with problem participants at meetings

Participant is: Overly talkative - to the extent that other participants do not have an opportunity to contribute.

Participant may be: An 'eager beaver,' exceptionally well informed; naturally wordy or nervous.

What to do: Interrupt with *'That's an interesting point ... Let's see what everyone else thinks.'* Directly call on others. Suggest *'Let's put others to work.'* When the person stops for a breath, thank him or her, restate the pertinent points and move on.

Participant is: Engaging in side conversations with others in the group.

Participant may be: Talking about something related to the discussion; discussing a personal matter or uninterested in the topic under discussion.

What to do: Direct a question to the person. Restate the last idea or suggestion expressed by the group and ask for the person's opinion.

Participant is: Argumentative – to the extent that others' ideas or opinions are rejected or others are treated unfairly.

Participant may be: Seriously upset about the issue under discussion; upset by personal or job problems; intolerant of others; lacking in empathy or is a negative thinker.

What to do: Keep your temper in check. Try to find some merit in what's said; get the group to see it too and then move on to something else. Talk to the person privately and point out what his or her actions are doing to the rest of the group. Try to gain the person's cooperation. Encourage the person to concentrate on positives, not negatives.

Participant is: Unable to express self so that everyone understands.

Participant may be: Nervous, shy, excited or not used to participating in discussions

What to do: Rephrase, restating what the person said, asking for confirmation of accuracy. Allow the person ample time to express his or herself. Help the person along without being condescending.

Participant is: Always seeking approval.

Participant may be: Looking for advice; trying to get leader to support his or her point of view or trying to put leader on the spot.

What to do: Avoid taking sides, especially if the group will be unduly influenced by your point of view.

Participant is: Bickering with other participant.

Participant may be: Carrying on an old grudge or feeling very strongly about the issue.

What to do: Emphasise points of agreement, minimise points of disagreement. Direct participants' attention to the objectives of the meeting. Mention time limits of the meeting. Ask participants to shelve the issue for the moment.

Participant is: Too quiet, unwilling to contribute.

Participant may be: Bored, indifferent, timid, insecure; more knowledgeable or experienced than the rest of the group.

What to do: Direct questions to the person that you're fairly sure s/he can respond to. Capitalise on the person's knowledge or experience by using them as a resource person.

Participant is: Seeking attention.

Participant may be: Feeling inferior or hiding a lack of knowledge by clowning around.

What to do: Keep reminding the person about the topic being discussed. Talk to the person privately. Point out what his or her actions are doing to the rest of the group.

Participant is: Uninvolved and unwilling to commit to new tasks.

Participant may be: Lazy; too busy already or feeling s/he should not have been asked to the meeting in the first place.

What to do: Ask for facts concerning the person's schedule. Ask the person to volunteer for tasks (others in group must as well). Make sure you ask the right people to future meetings.

Participant is: Already too over-committed to other things to take on new tasks.

Participant may be: Unaware of own skills and abilities or lacking in organisational skills.

What to do: Ask for facts concerning the person's schedule. Ask the person whether s/he is already over-committed. Tell the person you're counting on him or her. Send the person to a time-management seminar.

Participant is: A buck-passer who blames others for anything negative that happens and doesn't accept new tasks readily.

Participant may be: Unable to admit to making mistakes or afraid to take risks.

What to do: Make the person account for his or her actions. Ask for facts to back up allegations. Privately ask why the person won't accept new tasks.

Late start to meetings

'I waste a lot of time going to meetings. I'm always on time, but others just drift in. I have to chair a meeting myself but don't know how to make sure everyone come on time.'

You can make sure meetings start on time by:

1. Schedule meetings at odd times. A meeting scheduled to run from 10:15 - 11:00 am will get people's attention, especially if

previous meetings were scheduled for a full hour.

2. Start on time - no matter who's missing. If you don't - you set a too-casual tone.

3. Close the door at the appointed hour. This will stress the importance of starting on time and signal to latecomers that lateness is disruptive.

4. Cover the most important items first. If the significant business is discussed last, then timeliness is not as well rewarded as it should be. Plus, people are freshest at the meeting's start.

5. Items of interest to habitual latecomers should be raised early. Not to be nasty, but to motivate people to be there on time because there are things they want to hear about.

6. Speak privately to offenders. An occasional lapse doesn't merit a tongue-lashing. But a chronic lateness habit may be broken if you take the time to explain that it's not just a matter of enforcing the rules, it's that you value the person's input.

7. Make staff presentations part of meetings. Participation breeds greater enthusiasm. People tend to listen closely to their peers,

especially when they know that they too, will be speaking.

Why are some men intimidated by assertive women?

'I'm a new female manager and am running into resistance from the other male supervisors.'

How might a man feel if he's confronted by a woman in what he thinks of as male territory at work? Let's put this in another environment (away from the workplace):

Let's say a man's working in his backyard (workplace) and he spots a strange animal (a female manager) in his yard. This animal isn't like those he normally finds in these surroundings. He knows he's seen this type of animal in another environment (support position) but doesn't quite know how it will behave in the present situation. He's rightfully careful. He doesn't make any moves towards it (ignore the new female manager) and merely stands back, watching and studying it. If it shows anger or defensiveness toward him, he gets ready to defend himself. If it shows intimidation, he takes advantage of it.

This is the effect a woman has on a man when she enters a male-dominated work environment. The man doesn't know whether the woman is dangerous or not. She seems to be doing things - that to him - don't make sense. He has a hard time figuring her out. Naturally he reacts defensively!

Women entering supervisory or management positions need to understand these men's inner turmoil. Help them adapt to your presence (often unwanted) by earning their trust and respect. Don't expect immediate acceptance. It's been said that a woman not only has to be as good her as male counterparts, but she has to be better for her to be accepted as an equal or gain respect from male associates.

To continue with our hypothetical situation, the man is still standing back, studying the animal. He has his defences up, so that he's ready to protect himself if necessary. When the animal (the woman) makes funny sideways moves toward him (using feminine behaviour) he's even more wary.

Now the animal helps itself to some piece of food (part of his job) off his patio table. He's naturally annoyed. (This is what some women do - they do part of someone else's job thinking they're 'helping.')

In a home environment, women are conditioned to the idea that if she sees a task that requires action, she simply does it. In the workplace, this can step on the toes of other (mainly male) employees.

I could go on with this comparison, but I think you get my drift. Women *do* act differently when they're in supervisory or management positions.

A variety of things may cause men to be intimidated by an assertive woman. Heaven forbid, she may turn out to be better at supervision than he is! Some men who feel intimidated by women try every ploy to get rid of them. This type of man refers to all women in derogatory ways, by attempting to put them in their 'place.' For instance, they describe mentally strong women as, 'Pushy,' or 'Castrating.' On the other hand, most women are referred to as 'girls' and the majority of them haven't been 'girls' since they were thirteen years of age or so.

Male subordinates have another perceived problem. It's almost impossible for most of them to visualise themselves reporting to a woman. They think of women supervisors and managers as mother figures - and they're big boys now! They also might be intimidated by the fact that they don't know where women are coming from - they seem to play by a different set of rules. So how is a woman to deal with difficult male subordinates?

Here is how one new female supervisor dealt with this problem. Colleen was given a senior position, with several men reporting to her. One man objected because he had applied for her position. His behaviour bordered on insubordination and Colleen had to deal with it.

She said to him privately, *'I know you wanted my position, John and I can relate to how you must feel. I too know what it feels like to be overlooked for a promotion. I want and need your co-operation and I'll try to make it possible for us to work together harmoniously, but I won't tolerate any more negative behaviour from you. Can I count on you to change this?'*

John's behaviour improved and he became a productive employee. Later Colleen helped John identify why he had not been given her supervisory position. She was able to make sure he obtained the necessary training to equip him for the next promotional opportunity.

Staff object to my style of management

'I have difficulty supervising my male staff. They seem to ignore my instructions.'

Men are comfortable telling people what to do. If female supervisors request them to do a task, men believe they have the right to accept or refuse the woman's request. An example of this: A female supervisor wanted Mark to help Joe get a job done, so said, *'Joe looks as if he could use your help.'*

Mark replies, *'You're right he does seem to need help.'*

Later, the supervisor became upset when she found Joe still struggling along and learned that Mark had not offered to help. Mark thought that she was just making conversation, not asking him to help Joe. Because he had other, more pressing tasks to do, he'd thought her comment was not important.

The supervisor should have been clearer in her communication with Mark. She had supervised women in the past and that was the style of management that worked best with them. She didn't understand that men required a different kind of direction from her.

She should have stated, *'Mark, Joe needs help so I want you to leave the Miller report and help him until he completes his assignment.'* Mark would then know that she had prioritised Joe's project over the one he was working on and would have immediately helped Joe.

'It's difficult supervising my female staff. They accuse me of being too autocratic and demanding. How can I get them to do what I need them to do without offending them?'

Women supervise differently than men and don't like to pull rank, so they request, rather than demand. If a female supervisor uses a male type of supervisory method with women (ordering them to do tasks) the women feel as if the person is pulling rank and being bossy.

Dating colleagues and clients

'I'm trying to get over an office romance with my boss. Can you discuss office romances and explain whether you'd recommend them? What should I keep in mind for future possible office romances?'

It's amazing how fast colleagues catch on to the 'office romance.' You may think you've pulled the wool over everyone's eyes, but your body language will probably give you away and there will be subtle differences in how you interact with each other.

Most people believe that this kind of arrangement is fine - that it won't affect their chances of doing well with their company - but it does. Others may assume that any promotion you receive was because of your personal relationship with a person from upper management (should this be the case). It can be uncomfortable for co-workers throughout the romance because they may perceive that you are a pipeline to the upper level - and may tell about any difficulties they run into. They're also uncomfortable if and when the romance breaks up - and many don't know how to handle the situation. To be safe, stay clear of dating anyone you work with or have as a client. This is especially deadly if you work in the middle or upper management levels.

What causes or initiates most office romances? It's caused simply by proximity and availability to those of another gender. If they're doing basically the same kind of work - there can be a team spirit that can't always be matched by a spouse. How much time do you think most employees spend (awake) with their spouses? Married employees spend just about the same length of time (often more) with other sex colleagues as they spend with their spouses!

Occasionally office romances might work out - but the odds are that they won't. Beware of letting your hormones take over; think of the consequences should the romance break up. Inevitably, it will be difficult for both of you. When the romance sours and one of you decides to leave the company, more often than not, it's the woman, because she's likely in a more junior position. If neither employee goes, it will likely cause a serious strain on their office relationship with each other and with colleagues.

Dating Mentors

'A man I worked with became my mentor and lover. He helped me learn the ropes in our department, so I welcomed the advice he gave me. Our relationship went on for over two years, but I'm serious about my career and unfortunately our relationship went sour when I received a much-wanted and hard worked-for promotion. He seemed to be jealous of the progress I was making in our company. What

are some of the things I should be looking for in my next mentor?'

If the person you're having the romance with was your mentor, the break-up of the romance is bound to be even more traumatic. If you talk with successful employees, many will tell you that somewhere along the line they had a mentor (at least a part-time one).

A mentor is often an influential senior officer of the company s/he works for - who is possibly approaching retirement, but definitely committed to building the company by developing talented younger employees. They encourage what appear to be ordinary people to achieve success, because they see the hidden talent in these individuals. A mentor provides information and moral support to help younger employees through good and bad times. This person stops younger employees from making mistakes that they've seen others make. This allows their protégé to skip rungs in their promotional climb up the corporate ladder, but the mentor can 'pull them in' if the protégé is heading for trouble.

Unfortunately, male mentors for women are still a rare breed. Perhaps this is because such a relationship is still likely to attract gossip and speculation that sexual 'favours' may be part of the deal. However, if a man is willing to take this chance with his reputation, then the woman is encouraged to do so as well. For women, the pluses of having a mentor can far outweigh the minuses - unless there are sexual overtones mixed in with the help that's offered. Women should never accept the latter kind of 'help' up the ladder. The help they accept must have no strings attached!

There are many pluses to having a mentor, but occasionally there are negative sides as well. Because the mentor is often much older, they may not really be in touch with new technology or may retire while the protégé still needs assistance. Or, the mentor may have taken on a protégé for the wrong reasons - out of paternal or maternal feelings or to reinforce his or her own sense of power. Or the protégé may have been looking for a surrogate parent. Often a mentor may dump too many responsibilities and tasks on the protégé, who burns out and rebels, with negative consequences.

Watch that this person doesn't take over your life and make all the decisions for you. Listen to his or her advice, but remember that you should be the judge of whether to take that advice or not.

Should you date your mentor - decidedly *'No!'* The last thing you want to do is jeopardise your relationship by bringing romance into it. The break-up of this kind of romance can be very traumatic, especially for the protégé.

Occasionally, as a protégé progresses up the ladder, the mentor may become very critical of everything the protégé does. S/he can't seem to please the mentor - no matter what s/he does. The protégé could be getting too competent, therefore has become a threat to the mentor. The mentor reacts by making almost impossible demands. If this happens, the protégé must wean him or herself from the mentor. Very likely, they no longer need this kind of help anyway.

Fortunately, many mentors remain loyal and good friends - even when the protégé reaches the mentor's level. The protégé can now give the mentor peer support, which can be very valuable indeed.

Saboteur - or I'll go through the motions, but will fight you every step of the way!

'My secretary hates making coffee, but rather than admit this to anyone, she makes lousy coffee. One time she uses half a package of coffee, then one and a half packages, hoping that someone else will do the job.'

Obtain proof that she has done this. Ask her why she did what she did and explain your expectations. Tell her what the consequences will be if something similar happens in the future. Make sure this task is listed on her job description with standards of performance relating to how the coffee should be made.

Personality clashes

'One of my co-workers and I really don't get along, but when we're with others she pretends as if we do. How should I handle this kind of behaviour?'

Be gracious - she is trying her hardest to make the best of a bad situation. Say, *'I know you're not my greatest fan, so I appreciate your efforts to be friendly.'* This should at least let her know that you see she is trying to get along. You need to do the same. Communication is always a matter of give and take - make sure you're willing to give a little yourself to make the relationship more harmonious.

Always Slow

'We work in a team setting. A co-worker of mine is so slow completing her work that I wonder why she hasn't been fired. Sure she completes her reports, but it takes her so long to prepare it, I feel like taking over for her. She seems to have a low energy and often looks as if she's 'putting in time.' She's so disorganised that she's driving me to distraction because many of our projects are late.'

Her actions are affecting the entire team. Gain the other team members' assistance in confronting her. When parts of projects are allotted to team members, make sure she gives her word that she will have hers ready in time. Explain how disappointed you have been in the past when she has let the team down and explain that you're counting on her to do her share of the work. If she fails again say,

'We were counting on you to do your part. Can you explain why you have let us down again?'

If her actions continue, your team will have to discuss the matter with your supervisor (who obviously isn't on top of the issue).

Procrastinator

'I always get all the unpleasant tasks out of the way at the beginning of my day and feel good at the end of my workday. My co-worker puts these tasks off as long as possible and I see him getting testier as the day goes on because he still has to complete the disagreeable tasks. Why do people do this? They must know that this habit is adding to their stress level?'

There are two approaches to tackling distasteful tasks – doing them first or last. You've seen how effective the first way works, but obviously your colleague hasn't clued into this way of completing tasks. There may be several reasons why he puts things off.

One type of procrastinator says *'I'll do it tomorrow.'* They use passive resistance to get their way through game playing - the, *'If I put things off long enough, maybe they'll forget they asked me to do it.'* method. This is often the answer he'll give when he's snowed under with work. Or he may not have time to complete the task, but grudgingly accepts it anyway. He needs to stand up for himself if he finds himself with too many tasks to complete and how to say *'No'* when necessary.

Occasionally, the procrastinator is a perfectionist who believes he must be competent at everything he tries. If he isn't, he doesn't consider himself a worthwhile person. This is impossible to accomplish because of a constant fear of failure. This results in feelings of inferiority and the inability to live his life to the fullest.

He needs to learn how to enjoy the activity, rather than engaging in it solely for the results.

Employees, who consistently procrastinate when completing tasks, often find themselves the first ones fired. Companies simply can't afford to keep them on board. These employees look unprofessional, often become bottlenecks to others who are trying to get their work done and are a 'pain in the neck' to the more conscientious employees. Friends, family members and co-workers normally don't tolerate their excessive procrastination either.

How can you tell when procrastination becomes a problem? When people have something important to do, not much time to do it in, but find themselves looking for other activities to do instead. Or when *they* set deadlines and don't meet them! Procrastinators constantly delay making important decisions or work furiously at the last minute to complete crucial assignments.

There are five basic kinds of people who procrastinate more than average. Which type is your colleague?

The Hurry-up Type: He waits until the last minute and then works around the clock to meet deadlines. He needs to set concrete deadlines of when he must have tasks completed, giving a little leeway in case he runs into problems.

I'll Decide Tomorrow: He postpones decisions until events resolve the situation or others force a decision on him. He is normally a passive person who is a 'fence-sitter.'

Perfectionists: All tasks, no matter how small or insignificant he must complete faultlessly. He needs to select the tasks that are important and work hard at them. For the other assignments, he needs to know that it's okay ***not*** to do his best. When dealing with a perfectionist, identify for him when he can complete something in draft form. Let him know that you're not expecting perfection from him.

I'll Show Them! He delays tasks others give to him, as a way of retaining a sense of personal power and control. An employee does this when a supervisor delegates a task he doesn't think he should be doing.

Muddler: He puts off work because of bad habits, poor organisation or lack or direction. He goes around in ever widening circles, accomplishing little and always has an excuse about why he hasn't completed a task.

Which of the above describes your co-worker? Talk to him about what you've observed; help him see how his actions may be holding him back from a promotion and how procrastination can increase his stress level.

Lateness

'One of my colleagues is late for events she doesn't want to attend or is easily distracted and loses track of time. She disrupts meetings and lacks consideration for other people's valuable time. How can I tell her how annoying this is to others?

There are three basic kinds of time users. For instance, if there was a 2 pm appointment:

a. Person - arrives at exactly 2:00 pm.
b. Person - arrives at 1:50 pm (and gives the impression that she *just* made it!)

c. Person - arrives at 2:10 pm (and acts as if she's on time - gives no explanation for her lateness).

The type (a) person often cuts a fine line between being on time and being late. Occasionally, she slips into the (c) group. The (b) person's on time, but may arrive too early, so wastes valuable time while she waits. If she feels the need to be at least fifteen minutes early for an appointment, she should bring work with her to do while she's waiting.

The (c) person doesn't comprehend why others are hostile towards her and doesn't understand why those who're waiting are upset. By her actions, (coming in late) she's telling those who are waiting, that *their* time isn't important. She gives the impression that her time is more important, therefore it's all right for others to wait for her. Your colleague fits this category.

Explain how you feel when she's late (using feedback) and let her know why her behaviour is unacceptable to others and could result in disciplinary action from her supervisor.

Know it alls

'I have trouble dealing with the `know it all'
type of person who asks me for information,

then insists on giving me his/her version of what s/he believes is the answer.'

First, listen to their ideas. Then ask them for facts relating to their information (statistics, figures, etc.). Then, using information available to you, tell them the facts. Refer to rules, regulations, policies and procedure manuals or other written data if necessary. Most 'know-it-alls' can't back up their comments with hard facts and data.

Class Clown

'I don't need a company car often enough to have one of my own so use a car from the company car pool to visit my clients. Our company has a ruling that nobody is allowed to smoke in the cars and because I am a non-smoker that ruling is fine with me. However I seem to get one that reeks of smoke. I would like to refuse the car, but it is often the last one available. I know who smoked in the car. How should I deal with this?'

The person breaking the rules has all the attributes of a 'Class Clown.' He knows he was breaking the rules when he lit up, but refuses to stop smoking in the company cars. Whoever is in charge of allotting cars in the car pool should be informed of the problem. They are the ones who have the responsibility for dealing with the rule breaking. If that person refuses, talk to your supervisor.

Gossip

'A colleague of mine is forever interrupting my work with a juicy bit of gossip. I don't want to hear about her gossip and I've told her this several times. My resistance falls on deaf ears and before I know it, she's doing it again.'

Gossip is another form of indirect aggression. When people pass on gossip from one person to another it's inevitable that the meaning of the words changes somewhat from person to person. The person talking behind the back of the other person doesn't allow the person to defend him- or herself. For instance, a co-worker states, *'Did you hear about Carmen's husband? The police picked him up for drunk driving last night.'*

How should she deal with the gossiper? She should either ignore the comments or suggest to the person that they both talk to Carmen about the information. To stop the gossip, she'd say to Carmen, *'I thought you should know there's a rumour going around that the police charged your husband with drunk driving last night. Were you aware of the rumour?'*

This lets Carmen know there *is* a rumour. You wouldn't ask Carmen whether it's true - you'd just let her know what's happening. The giver of the gossip soon learns that they won't get away with talking behind others' backs. It also stops gossipers from passing on unwanted gossip to this person.

There's also another serious issue here. While you are gossiping, you are wasting company time and money. If observed by upper management, it could keep you from receiving a promotion and you wouldn't even know why!

Sticky-Iffies (Backhanded compliments)

'The man I work with is forever giving me backhanded compliments such as, 'You earn a lot for a woman.' This isn't a one-time thing and he does it with everyone. Am I being too sensitive? How should I respond?'

He's giving you a compliment and then ends up giving you a put down. This discounts the positive statement, because he adds something negative to his comment as well. He's probably using these disguised or obvious put downs to hurt others. When dealing with him, use the following tactics:

1. After receiving the sticky-iffy or put down, reflect your understanding of the situation. Say, *'You feel ... think ... believe ...'* which confirms that you heard what they said to you (a form of paraphrasing).
2. Then state, *'I understand ... perceive ... appreciate ... empathise with ... realise ...'* then express *their* point of view as you perceive it.
3. State, *'I think ... feel ... believe ... have ...'* and state *your* beliefs about the topic. Don't start your statement with such words as but, however, although or nevertheless.
4. Ask an open question (one that can't be answered by a 'yes' or a 'no.').

For example you would treat a discriminatory statement regarding gender:

He says, *'You're earning a good salary for a woman.'*

She says, *'You believe that women should earn less than men?'*

He says, *'Yes, I do.'*

You say, *'I appreciate what you're saying. I believe women deserve an equal chance to earn the same kind of salary as men. Women pay rent like men, pay the same for food as men and pay taxes like men. What are the reasons for your belief that women should earn less than men?'*

An example relating to age: They say,

'You're pretty young to be a supervisor aren't you?'

You say, *'You feel that I'm too young to be a supervisor?'*

They say, *'Well you are young!'*

You say, *'I realise that I'm young. I have six years' experience in this department, have a B.A. degree and have completed all the supervisory training provided by my company. What other prerequisites do you feel I need to handle my position?'*

An example relating to racial slurs:

They say, *'Every time I take a taxi, it's always people from Asia who are driving. Can't you people find anything else to do, except drive a taxi?'*

You say, *'You feel that people from Asia should have jobs other than driving a taxi. I realise why you must believe that. Many people from my country have to get extra education to work at their usual occupations in your country, so become taxi drivers in the interim. I'm taking university courses and will soon be working in my normal type of occupation. What kind of special courses did you take to work in your occupation?'*

An example relating to a person's size:

They say, *'You're in pretty good shape for a man your size.'*

You say, *'You think that because I'm a smaller man, that I'm not strong?'*

They say, *'Well, you are small to be able to lift that big barbell.'*

You say, *'I can see how you could come up with that perception. I'm sixty years old now and have been lifting weights since I was fifteen. I've won several weight-lifting contests and still work out every day. Can you see why I'm in good shape for a man my size?'*

Your tone of voice is very important in these exchanges. Your voice should not show defensiveness, but should state facts. This starts a dialogue where you can discuss facts rather than emotions. Use this technique for any sticky-iffy comments, disguised or obvious put downs.

Held back from promotion

'I've tried everything I know to get ahead in my company, but it seems as if they are reluctant to put women into management or senior positions in my company. How can I get the kind of job I know I can handle?'

Many women (often sole breadwinners) struggle to escape the pink-collar ghetto by obtaining supervisory or management positions. Here are some suggestions that may help you progress up the corporate ladder:

Step 1: Decide *where* you want to go by obtaining career counselling. Then investigate *how* you can get where you want to go. Will this be through on-the-job training or do you require formal education and/or training? Once you determine this, obtain that training, possibly while working at a junior-level position in the field of your choice.

Step 2: Document every task you do in your present position. Determine whether you're doing an important part of your boss's work. Look for those tasks that require independent action and/or decision-making on your part.

You'll find that if you can identify the decisions you now make, you may be able to convince your employer that you're capable of making more major ones. You'll just be using different kinds of data. Look for duties where your judgement was crucial to the outcome of a task. Look for clear-cut areas of responsibility, authority and accountability. In other words, look for things you do on a regular basis in which *you* decide the outcome. These are the skills that those in management positions require and you'll be well paid for using them.

Step 3: Ask your boss if your talents could be utilised in other areas of his or her department. Explain that you're willing to take a cut in salary if necessary. Even a junior position (as long as it has a toehold on the bottom rung of the promotional ladder) is better than a support or clerical one.

If your boss doesn't think this is a good idea, talk to someone in your Human Resources Department. Identify the decision-making qualities you've developed and what specialty you would like to get into. Ask them to let you know about any positions that arise that would utilise your qualifications.

As backup, watch for job postings on your company's bulletin board and be sure to apply for positions you believe you can handle. Have the Human Resources Department explain why you're not suitable for the vacancies you're rejected for. This may be hard at first, but they'll explain where you need to improve your qualifications.

Step 4: Talk with someone in a high position in your company who's eager to see women progress in business and ask his or her advice about what kinds of experience or education you're lacking.

Step 5: When responding to ads, stay clear of those that describe the position or the candidate with words such as 'skills, right arm, high-class, bright, achiever, hard working, support services, assistant to or pleasant working conditions,' etc. These denote lower-level positions. Watch instead for words such as 'self-starter, career-oriented, challenging position,' etc.

Most senior positions identify their salary ranges as annual salaries - intermediate in monthly salaries and junior positions by hourly or weekly wages.

Step 6: Ask senior women in the company to help you reach your goal. Most of them will be glad to help you. Ask them how they got where they are and the route they took to get there. The saying, *'It's not what you know, but **who** you know,'* still plays an important part in being promoted.

- Once you reach a higher position, here are some ideas that will help you succeed. Know your position duties and do them well. Always have areas you have to learn when accepting a new position. If you already feel you know all the duties of the job - you're probably overqualified already. If you resign from a position, never burn your bridges and badmouth your former company, boss or co-workers. You never know, ten years down the road when there's been a full turnover of staff, you may learn about a 'plumb' job, but won't be considered if they check your personal record and find 'sour grapes.'

- Make sure you receive equal training and educational opportunities as your peer group. At management meetings, when everyone's eyes rivet on you at coffee

213

break, simply state '*I take cream and sugar.*'

- If asked to take minutes at a management meeting, get your personal assistant, explaining that you can't participate properly when taking notes. Learn to control your emotions such as anger, anxiety and fear (never use tears to get your way!). Be willing to express your ideas to your boss in private, but never criticise or challenge him or her in public.

- Never date a colleague or client you deal with on a regular basis.

- Know how your company deals with expense accounts (and don't always go bargain-express).

- Don't put yourself down. Learn from your mistakes and try to do better the next time. Learn the proper way to accept compliments for a job well done.

- If your boss is weak and indecisive - ask for written guidelines that identify where you have the authority to make decisions on your own. Explain that this is so that your boss isn't 'bothered' with trivial details. Not only will you be making more decisions, but your boss may be glad to toss them to you.

- Don't verbalise high personal ambitions to colleagues (especially men). Discuss this only with your supervisor or Human Resources representative. The time you should explain your full career plans, is during your interview and you're asked the question *'What are your career plans?'*

Freezes under pressure

'One of my colleagues freezes whenever an emergency situation happens at work. He becomes immobilised – frozen to the spot. He also stays away from work if he's expected to make important decisions, so others are forced to make those decisions. In group situations he becomes mute and seems unable to speak. What's happening here?'

When his fight or flight response kicks in, instead of either fighting or running away from the danger, he simply freezes. He doesn't make decisions because he's afraid he'll make the wrong one. This again immobilises him. He becomes speechless because he seems to be highly prone to stage fright.

His behaviour is very passive, so suggest that he take an assertiveness training course. Help him learn how to make decisions. When he's forced to make a decision talk to him privately and ask him, *'What do you think you should do? Why did you make that decision? What other alternatives are open to you?'* If you're the one needing him to make the decision - give him deadlines and check with him along the way to see if he needs more information before making his decision.

These sound like well entrenched behaviours that may require professional help to overcome. He's likely had some pretty horrific situations in his past that have caused his immobilisation.

Bashful

'Sam is so shy that it's painful to watch him interact with others. The least little thing causes him to blush beet red, to perspire heavily and stammer his words. His colleagues and friends react by being super-careful while they're around him. Others evade him because of the guilt they feel when they inadvertently make him respond with this kind of behaviour.'

Bashful people readily show that they're greatly embarrassed by their non-verbal signals. They have nightmares about situations they might face the next day and by the time the situation occurs, they've worked themselves up until they're almost immobilised. These people are prone to a lot of teasing from stronger individuals and suffer terribly. To overcome: follow the steps for 'Freezes under pressure.'

Self beraters

'One of my colleagues relentlessly puts herself down. She acts as if everything that's gone wrong must be her fault and is highly critical of her work and actions. She seeks daily reassurance from others that she's doing a good job and needs others to give praise for her actions (whether it's earned or not.)'

Most self beraters are average performers but they almost beg others to find fault with everything they do. They try to avoid receiving hurt from others by identifying their own faults, before anyone else can do it for them. If you decide to help her, she'll need a confidant who won't criticise, but will provide empathy. Help her realise what she's doing to herself with her constant self put-downs. Explain how others lose faith in her ability when she keeps running herself down. Your colleague desperately needs praise and recognition when her assignments go well. Make sure you provide this for her.

Uninvolved

'When it's time to go to lunch and I ask a colleague where she wants to go for lunch, her standard answer is, 'I don't care - wherever you want to go is fine with me.' I've tried to encourage her to state her preference, but still get the same response. Then, no matter where we go, she grumbles about the food or the service! How should I handle this?'

Start by using feedback to describe what her actions are doing to you and others when she plays games like she does. She probably isn't even aware that she's doing so, but there's a method to this madness. The deliberately uninvolved person is never wrong, but is never right either. She may say she doesn't care which decision is made, but her body language shows otherwise.

In the future, insist that she clearly states what she wants to do for lunch - that silence or *'I don't care - wherever you want to go is fine with me ...,'* is unacceptable. If she still won't state her opinion, say, *'So you don't care which restaurant we go to?'* Then point out that you don't want any grumbling about the food or service.

Sham assertive

'One would never know it by his behaviour, but Bill detests me. In private conversations he lets me know how he feels, but if anyone else is around, he's as nice as pie to me. I've recently learned that he's spreading lies about me.'

People in this category have problems in any but the most superficial relationship. They may seem open, assertive, warm and even extroverted, but this covers for a lack of honesty. Start by saying, *'I know you're not my greatest fan, so I appreciate your efforts to be friendly when others are around. What I don't like are the stories you're telling about me behind my back. If you have a beef with me - tell it to my face, so I'll have a chance to deal with it.'* Be polite and courteous with him at all times, but don't let your guard down. He could still be badmouthing you behind your back.

Bootlickers

'I'm rather amused at the games people play to get on the right side of their bosses. They fawn over them, giving passes to sporting events and

doing special favours for their bosses. These things have nothing to do with work - so why do they do it except to curry favour with their bosses? I refuse to do this and am wondering if it is holding me back at work.'

These individuals are observed preening before entering their boss's office - doing up their suit jackets, slicking their hair, correcting their posture. Some resort to becoming the office tattle-tale - telling their boss all the gossip. They're manipulators who want to be noticed but use the wrong means.

Concentrate on your own behaviour instead of confronting bootlickers. You don't have to resort to the underhanded and ingratiating actions of a bootlicker. Instead, concentrate on doing the best job you can - so your boss looks good. Help your boss by keeping him/her informed about company issues s/he might have missed.

If you must speak to the bootlicker, take him/her aside and ask why s/he indulges in playing this game and what s/he expects to gain from it. Then explain your own aversion to that kind of behaviour.

Over-committers - Renegers

'Bob always has a smile and a friendly word to share and people instantly like him. However he promises that whatever you want from him - you'll get - then lets you down and doesn't deliver on his promises. I'd hate to hurt his feelings, but this kind of shirking of duty has to stop. I need to count on him when he says he's going to do his share of the work.'

Let him know that you're counting on him to do what he's promised to do. Say, *'You've let me down in the past by promising to do tasks you didn't have time to do. I'm counting on you to do this. If there's any chance that you can't deliver - I need to know now - not later when it's too late.'*

He may also need to know when you're happy with his performance. After all, he's trying to please others, but gets himself in over his head in the process, so may need reassurance that you're pleased with his work.

Other overcommitted people are prone to giving extravagant praise so they can use you. They believe if they constantly say things designed to please you (greatly exaggerating reality) you'll do as they ask. They're afraid their plan, procedure, policy or assignment can't stand on its own merit, so they use unwarranted praise to gain acceptance of them.

These are nice people who can't say *'No'* to others' requests. However they often find they haven't time to do what they promised. They make promises they expect to fulfil or they mislead you by breaking promises they hadn't planned to keep in the first place. They love harmony and hate to argue, so they'll agree to do what others ask them to do. They avoid confrontation hoping they won't hurt others' feelings. They promise too much or say they'll do something they don't really want to do. Unable to handle it all, they put off action or making decisions and break their promises. They don't hurt others intentionally, but often cause difficulty for others who are depending on them to follow-through.

Have him give either a verbal (in public if possible) or written commitment to you that he will complete the task. When necessary - you make the decision whether he does the task or not. If he does commit herself, explain that you're counting on him to follow-through. Let him know the consequences should he let you down in the future.

Stalking Co-worker

'One of my co-workers began pursuing me two months ago. I'm not attracted to her and let her know that I'm not interested in a relationship. She hasn't been obvious, but I often see her watching me at work. What is of concern to me, is that I have seen her parked outside my apartment several times and have run into her at the supermarket too many times for it to be an accident. How can I get her to stop doing this?'

This is a case of stalking. Start by documenting every time you notice her stalking you. If others have observed her behaviour, have them document their observations as well. Then talk to her - giving her a copy of your documentation. Explain that her behaviour must stop. If it doesn't, speak to your Human Resources manager and/or union representative to have them speak to her about her unacceptable behaviour. If she still persists - speak to the police and obtain their advice on how you should be dealing with this situation.

Email abuses

'One of my colleagues is forever sending me smutty jokes over the internet. We have a

company policy relating to this, but I'm reluctant to make a fuss.'

Make a copy of the company email policy and email it to this person. Explain that by accepting the unacceptable email, you are just as guilty. If the jokes continue to arrive, show your manager a copy of some of the offending emails and your request to have them stopped.

Chapter 4

UNHAPPY AT WORK

I hate my job!

'I'm so unhappy at work that I have to force myself to go to work every morning. It's because of management problems - they don't seem to care anything about their employees!'

Companies do many things to make life miserable for their staff and must be diligent to remove as many employee frustrations as they can. Some employees are de-motivated by companies who:

Use restrictive supervision

You'll likely obtain less job satisfaction if your supervisor gives you little chance to take an active part in how you complete your assignments. The more employees participate in *how* they do things, the more co-operative they will be.

The supervisor, who uses an authoritarian leadership style, is setting him/herself up to fail. If you have one of these supervisors, try feedback to alleviate the problem. If your supervisor won't listen, you may have to suffer for a while until a promotion's available. Other alternatives are; take a lateral move to another department or as a last resort, leave the company.

Lack of recognition

Supervisors de-motivate staff if they identify only what their subordinates do *incorrectly*. They should concentrate instead on what they do *correctly*, which will encourage better performance. When correcting behaviour, instead of saying *'You made a mistake'* they should say, *'The next time you do this, I'd like you to do it this way.'*

In the 'Old School of Management,' supervisors believed it was their *right* to take credit for any new ideas suggested by their subordinates. As expected, this just de-motivates employees and discourages any new ideas. Progressive supervisors are learning that if they give employees credit where credit's due, their staff is motivated to perform better. This also alleviates mediocrity and marginal production. Possibly, your supervisor isn't aware of how de-motivating his/her actions are. Use feedback to explain how his/her lack of giving recognition is affecting you.

Monotonous work

When companies implement 'job rotation' for their employees, they are attempting to make employees' jobs more interesting. Job rotation involves several employees who work at substantially the same class or level of work and pay range. Employers who use job rotation reap extra benefits because people can fill more than one job. Don't knock your company if they're doing this. They *are* trying to keep your work interesting. If they aren't; suggest they try it!

Little opportunity to try new ideas

Another prime de-motivater occurs when supervisors refuse to listen to their staff when they try to explain better, faster or more efficient ways of completing their work. They'll likely listen if you use comparisons, identify the advantages/disadvantages of both the new and the old ways and identify the cost savings of your proposed new method.

No new skill growth

At one time, companies spent training dollars on their people and still couldn't keep up with the demand for competent qualified people. Recently companies have had to tighten their training budgets. Companies may refuse to give training that they believe employees can't use right away. Employees whose promotions are six months to one year away may find it difficult to obtain preparatory training.

Employees, who find themselves in this position, would be wise to obtain and pay for this training themselves. This will ensure they *are* ready for the next step up (without their company having to put out the training money). This gives the employee an edge over competitors for the position who have not obtained this training on their own. These training dollars are well spent and a good investment by the employee. Often employers will reimburse such expenditures for related training if the training occurred while the employee was in another position in the company.

Poor fit between abilities and job requirements

Before the economic downturn, many employees projected that they would climb the ladder in their companies very quickly. Many find they're over qualified for their present positions with little chance to move up in the company. If the expected promotion is still far in the future, they may be forced to move on to another company.

Anger expressed at work

'I have an employee whose productivity has plummeted. I know the problem doesn't stem from a personal or family problem, but the quality of her work has got to improve. How can I find out what's going on?'

Your first step is to have an interview with her and ask the reasons for her poor performance. Be prepared with facts to back up your belief about her work. You may find the following reasons behind her behaviour:

Direct 'Take that:'

Usually a person's first response to a negative working condition is to directly attack it. Often this leads to very productive and creative effort. New procedures can develop this way. 'Necessity is the mother of invention,' so some frustration can be desirable. However, if the blocking condition doesn't yield, she may openly show expressions of hostility, destructive in intent or she may use less direct methods.

Example: A manager fails to recognise an employee's ability to come up with new ideas.

The employee quits giving new ideas. The employee knows how she can do a faster, better job but becomes frustrated because she can't complete a task her own way. She could become a 'middle of the road' employee with tunnel vision.

Sabotage - 'Let's get back at Them:'

Sabotage in the work-setting usually takes a much milder form than we typically associate with this word. Yet subtle forms of sabotage are very common. The work slowdown, the omitted procedure and the small 'error,' are all evidence of the frustration/anger model at work.

Example: A personal assistant intentionally makes lousy coffee, because she doesn't drink coffee and feels coffee-making should not be her responsibility.

Turning inward - 'It must be me!'

One of the most pathetic results of prolonged frustration is the tendency on the part of some to turn their anger inward upon themselves. Instead of venting their anger against the blocking conditions through direct or indirect means, such as already listed, the individual begins to attack him or herself and winds up with a feeling of 'I'm no good'. Turning such a person around is a management challenge of major magnitude.

Example: Employees who've taken risks and have been 'burned' may retreat into themselves and refuse to make decisions - use tunnel vision when completing assignments, won't take risks and must feel safe in any decision they make. Those who have written warnings on their file or who have been reprimanded in public will also react this way.

Over-Compliance 'If that's what you want..:'

One excellent way of expressing anger at the blocking boss, is to do exactly what s/he asks regardless of the circumstances. The boss can't fault this practice, because after all, it's what s/he said, but s/he didn't mean to be taken so literally. Often when a union wants to make life difficult for management, the union starts going by the letter, rather than the spirit of the contract.

Example: You've given an employee a set of instructions on how to complete a project, you assume she will use her common sense and add pertinent information as necessary to complete the assignment. She doesn't, so the report is useless.

Emotional withdrawal - 'You aren't that important:'

One way to deal with continuing frustration is to deny the importance of the blocking conditions. This is the familiar 'sour grapes' attitude. We often see employees become apathetic and just 'go through the motions' on the job, by their actions saying, this job isn't that important; the really important things for me are outside the job. Productivity gains would be considerable if the interest and energy many workers spend on becoming star bowlers could be rekindled on the job.

Example: An employee follows her job description to a 'T.' As her manager, you know she's capable of much more.

How to improve job satisfaction and productivity

So, how can you keep your employee wanting to contribute and be more productive?

1. Provide an atmosphere of approval:

a) An atmosphere of approval can be created by taking the following steps:

- o Recognise the importance of employee suggestions.
- o Listen to them – if not now, arrange to do so later.
- o Avoid Progress Killers such as: *'We've always done it this way!'*
- o Tell why their new ideas won't work. If employee gives a good idea, implement it as soon as possible and make sure you give the employee credit for the idea.

2. *Allow them meaningful participation:*

The evidence is pretty convincing that whenever people can influence their own work in a way that provides them with an opportunity to have a decisive voice, they will be more interested and involved. Employees will feel their participation is meaningful if you practice the following:

a) Analyse *your* job and decide which tasks can be moved downward. If the task is easy for you to do - it can likely be delegated.

b) Be willing to take the risk of more job involvement by your subordinates.

c) Encourage your employees to volunteer for assignments they feel they can handle.

d) Don't con your employees with the feeling that they're giving meaningful participation when a decision has already been made.

e) When your decision has been influenced by the employee's ideas tell him or her.

3. *Performance Feedback:*

Some managers (and thank goodness they're getting fewer and fewer) believe that the yearly performance appraisal is all that's necessary for the employee to perform properly. Of course, along the way they believe that the employee must be corrected if s/he does something wrong, but otherwise they're 'on their own'. Employees that work for this kind of manager find:

a) They don't have an up-to-date, accurate job description of the tasks they're expected to perform - and how they are to be performed.

b) They aren't sure what's expected of them - therefore have no set objectives to meet.

c) They seldom hear about what they did right (except silence), but appear to hear lots about what they did wrong.

4. *Consistent discipline:*

If managers show favouritism or have a personality clash with employees, consistent discipline is usually a mirage. To ensure consistent discipline a manager must:

a) Review rules and standards periodically to evaluate their relevancy to current situations.
b) Ensure that employees know company rules and regulations.
c) Reward or punish consistently.
d) Be aware of extenuating circumstances.
e) Document your action and the reasoning you used to make decision.
f) Follow-up to see if the situation has improved.

5. *Right of appeal:*

This is used only after serious attempts have been made by both the supervisor and the employee to settle a dispute. The third person (the mediator) is often a Human Resources specialist, a union representative or any other trained negotiator who can remain objective about the conflict. Companies that don't offer the 'Right of

Appeal' (which are usually non-union firms) are missing a very effective management tool. Managers are advised as follows:

a) You're not always right. Appeal procedures protect your people from your occasional lapses into biased opinion.

b) Be sure to listen effectively to your employee's reasoning behind their actions.

c) If you and your employee can't agree, involve another impartial third party.

d) Be willing to change your mind.

e) Welcome this appeal method as an aid, not a threat. Remember, you too will have access to this management tool!

Consider these ideas and see if they don't change your employee's productivity.

Mid-Life Crisis

Have you found yourself thinking, *'Is this all there is?'* If so, it's possible that you're trapped on a mid-life plateau in either your marital/family situation or due to the type of work you're doing. It's easy to get into a rut and stay there. So, if your marital or family situation is the problem - what could you do to put some spark back into your life? Or is the situation serious enough to consider family or marital counselling? If so, make that a priority for you to investigate and soon. Life is too short to waste life being happy.

Did work used to be exciting, but you now find it and your life to be boring you to tears? Every morning you get up and go to work, then come home? When you get home it's the same old routine - you read the paper, eat dinner, do some work, watch TV and go to bed. Then you get up and do it all again.

What are you going to do with the rest of your life? You hate the thought that your work is going to be like this forever, but you don't know how to break out of the rut or are afraid of failing in new ventures. If you're saying any of the above - you've plateaued (not going anywhere) and likely feel trapped. If you can accept that you're at the end of a phase, you can begin planning a new one.

For many of us, work is the basis of our identity and self-esteem - which is fine, as long as we're successful. But promotions do eventually cease, sometimes provoking a terrible sense of failure. Mastery of the work also may bring feelings of tedium. Dentists tire of filling molars, teachers become bored with their students and lawyers get weary of divorce courtrooms.

When this happens there's a good chance lethargy will set in; the person's productivity lessens and the joy of going to work ceases. Life becomes a tedious task - not a rewarding experience. Although different strategies work for different people, there are courses of action that can take them off that plateau. Here are some ways to leave it behind you and help you get on with your life.

Using skills in a different way

Plateaued people, who are unable to change their jobs, can benefit by using their knowledge and skills in different ways. One way is to be a mentor to younger people in your organisation. Being a mentor involves the challenge of being the wise teacher. Middle age is more likely to be a period of personal renaissance, especially if you encourage the creativity and growth of younger people. You'll create a new way to earn self-respect and will continue to challenge your abilities.

Another challenge is to become involved in your community and/or government. The volunteer sector can be as gratifying as your professional work, if you approach it with the same kind of commitment. Those who participate in the community, gain the opportunity of wrestling with different issues, having hands-on experience, being creative, exerting leadership and making a visible difference in society. It's another place where you can use your leadership and wisdom to help others.

Why do so many people find themselves in the wrong type of occupation? The following shows percentages of why people get off the track with their careers.

Reasons people choose the wrong career

1. They follow the advice of others instead of using their own instincts - 30%
2. Blind themselves to what the job will *really* be like - 25%
3. Assume they can live with a lower salary than they're used to - 20%
4. Don't check out potential problems and issues during their employment interview - 15%
5. Don't obtain career counselling.

Therefore, it's very important that you investigate the following:

1. Understand yourself - your wants, needs and desires.
2. Know what career options are open and available to you.
3. Know how to choose a suitable career path by evaluating your transferrable skills
4. Know where you can obtain the education and/or training you need to enter a new career.

Plateaued people often say, *'I do my job and just hope that something else will turn up.'* Those who work in large organisations are especially prone to being 'good' - waiting for the good fairy to notice them and reach out with a magic wand. However, if you wait for superiors (or fate) to create opportunities, you give others far too much power over your life. It's your responsibility to say what you want. You know your competencies better than anyone else. You're in a unique position to make a case for yourself, to change the design of your work, so that it's more challenging.

Think about the aspects of your work that give you intrinsic satisfaction and then enlarge on them. Speak to your supervisor or Human Resources Department about the steps you've taken to prepare yourself for your chosen career path. Make sure they know you're serious and want an opportunity to change careers. While you're unlikely to get everything you want, you're more likely to get something, than you are if you didn't speak up.

When I was working as a Human Resources Manager, a young woman came to me and explained that she was at the top of her clerical level and wanted to know what kinds of promotional opportunities were available to her within our company. I asked her where *she* wanted to go - what occupation she had chosen. She replied, *'I don't really care what occupation I get into, as long as it's a promotion and brings me more money.'*

I explained that she had gone as far as she could go as a generalist - that now she'd have to specialise. She still didn't appear to understand what I meant, so I suggested alternate careers. *'Are you interested in marketing, computers, human resources, accounting, sales, operations, production or any other specialty area?'* The woman just shrugged her shoulders and repeated her original statement about salary.

She failed to understand that companies don't just offer jobs to people; she needed to do something to show her interest, aptitude and ability in the career she'd chosen. This woman should have prepared herself for promotional opportunities, rather than expecting her company to 'find' the opportunities for her. For instance: If she decided that she wanted to work her way up to a purchasing manager's position, she should have taken the initiative and enrolled in related courses. She could have taken these in the evening so she would be ready for the next junior buyer position that became available.

I sent her away to think about the area she wished to pursue, but never heard from her again - it was too much trouble for her to do this 'work' herself. She was unaware that I could have placed her into junior positions in most of the areas I'd identified.

When I was climbing the corporate ladder in Human Resources, I ran into a 'Catch-22' situation. I had asked my company if they would pay for the costs of supervisory training so I'd be ready for a pending supervisory position. Their reply was, *'We can't pay for that kind of training for you, because you're not a supervisor.'*

242

I debated whether I could afford to pay for the training. Because I was serious about being considered for this type of position, I took the initiative and registered for a six-week supervisory course that I could take in the evenings. When my company posted the expected supervisory position, I spoke to the manager in the area about applying for the position. His reply is still etched in my memory when he stated, *'We can't consider you for that kind of a position, because you don't have supervisory training!'*

I'd been prepared for this eventuality and produced a copy of my certificate of training. Because of this and my relevant experience with the company, they reluctantly hired me for the supervisory position: and became the first woman appointed to such a position in their company. If I hadn't taken the initiative, I'd likely still be in a clerical or low-paying position.

The amount I invested in this training has been repaid one hundred times over. So if lack of training is your problem, pay for it yourself. If your answer is that you can't afford the costs - you're making excuses. Have a garage sale or do without other non-essentials. The bizarre thing is, that my company reimbursed me for the cost of my training because it was training they would have paid for anyway after I obtained the position!

Career Decisions

There are five different types of career decisions a person could make in their lifetime:

1. Choosing an occupation.
2. Choosing a job.
3. Choosing an educational program (of study or training).
4. Choosing a career path (a series of jobs, occupations and educational programs leading to a career goal).
5. Choosing how to spend a period of time (what to do next week, month, year, etc. This type of career decision often encompasses several other types of career decisions.)

Whatever decision you make - do it! Don't wait for your employer or something external to trigger your response. If you need career counselling - get it and spend some time deciding what you want to do with the rest of your life.

Are you ready for a promotion?

Companies shouldn't promote employees simply because they've done well in their present position, but only if they can handle a higher level of responsibility. Employers will ask themselves the following questions before considering you for a promotion. See if you're ready:

Are you competent in your present position?

a) If you're not a solid performer in your present position, were you in the wrong position to begin with?

b) Would you excel in the new position, because you'll be able to use your transferrable skills? Or,

c) Is it possible that you're not ready for a promotion?

d) How well have you prepared yourself for the next promotional level?

e) Do you really know the responsibilities of the new position you're aiming for?

f) Will you need more training to prepare you for that promotional opportunity?

Have you shown your employer that you're serious?

Have you gone through career counselling, decided where you want to go and shown your employer you're serious about your ambitions? If necessary, have you registered in courses that will help you progress in your chosen career?

Can you communicate effectively?

If you can't get along with co-workers, clients and bosses, you'll likely stay where you are and not be considered for a promotion. You'll be communicating with others for the rest of your life and will be living with a life-long handicap unless you make this one of your primary goals. Take public speaking courses so you can say what you want to say, when you want to say it.

Are you a long-term investment?

Companies may be reluctant to hire you if they perceive you're a job-jumper. They'll want to recoup any money they spend on training for you, so they'll be looking for stability on your part. Let your employer know that you're serious about your career choice.

Are you a good role model?

If you had your choice, would you be willing to work for someone like yourself? What faults do you have? Are you prepared to work on your faults and improve them? Do others respect you and accept your ideas as valid (or do you have to fight all the way to get your ideas accepted)? If the latter is the case, you may need to work on your interpersonal skills.

Will you be supervising others?

If you've never supervised others before, make sure you obtain supervisory training *before* asking for a promotion. Get the training and put yourself ahead of some of your competitors who want the same promotional opportunities.

Are you ready to be a supervisor?

Some people never make good supervisors. For instance, if you're the top salesperson for your department, think twice before accepting a supervisory position. You require a new set of pre-requisites if you're a supervisor. Typically, sales people hate paperwork and sales supervisors have to do a lot of paperwork. Sales people love dealing with a variety of people, having challenges and meeting sales quotas. Sales supervisors may find themselves tied to an office or a desk and may miss the lively interaction with their clients.

Choosing the right career for you is very important, not only when your work life begins, but later on in life as well. Remaining flexible is a must, for success.

The rewards of choosing the right career

Those who work at a suitable career find life tremendously stimulating. Somehow they find that their work generates its own momentum, which brings extraordinary satisfaction to the person. These fortunate people can't wait to get up in the morning and start their days running. Mondays for these individuals, are outstanding. Those with this attitude towards work, find they have a much better chance of progressing within their chosen careers.

On the other hand, some have difficulty making decisions and wait for outside forces to initiate changes in their lives. I always say, *'The only thing you get by fence-sitting is slivers.'* If you're one of these fence-sitters, remember that your indecisiveness can raise your stress level considerably. You can probably recall a time when you waited and waited before making a decision and can likely recall the relief you felt when you finally got off the fence and made a decision. So, get off that fence and start making decision about where you want to go with your life! There are answers to this dilemma, but you must be willing to invest time, effort and dedication to turn things around.

Many people go through the 'blahs' when they reach thirty-five or forty. They make such comments as, *'Is this all there is?'* They've probably reached many of their personal and career goals and find life very dull and uninteresting. This likely happens because they haven't had another goal on the 'back burner' ready to kick in when they came close to achieving their present goal.

Some workers are forced into setting career goals because they've been let go from a position (either laid off or fired). For some, this becomes a true blessing in disguise, because they're forced to look at their lives and make serious plans about where they want to go. For some, it might be the first time they've really asked themselves what they want to do with their career lives.

Goal setting takes a lot of effort, dedication and time, but *it's worth it!* If it takes two years for you to decide where you want to go, that's okay, as long as you're steadily working towards finding the right career for you. Don't attempt something unless you really want to succeed at it. There are too many competitors out there - people who know where they want to go and how they're going to get there.

The big question for many is how to find their ideal career. Most find this when they obtain professional career counselling. I find that those with the mid-life career blahs can feel frustrated and depressed, but as soon as they find a new channel for their abilities and talents, their outlook improves immediately. You might consider looking at the career counselling service we offer by going to: www.dealingwithdifficultpeople.info/unique-career-counselling-service

Overlooked for a promotion

Consider this situation. There's a promotional position in your company that you've applied for because you believe you're well qualified for it. You submit your resume for consideration and learn that someone else has been hired for the position. You *know* this person is less qualified than you, so you're upset. What steps should you take? How should you approach this situation? Is it too late to do something about it? No, it isn't. But simply complaining to the hiring supervisor or saying, *'How come you hired somebody who's less qualified than I?'* is not likely to work.

Instead, phone the supervisor who was in charge of hiring and ask for fifteen minutes of his time (we'll assume that it's a man). If he asks why, explain that it's important for you to obtain some information regarding the position. He'll have his guard up, but if you're persistent he'll see you. He expects you to attack him and will be on the defensive, even before you enter the room. So your approach has to be more subtle. (The hard-nosed approach of most labour negotiations won't work in this situation.)

You could start by being honest and admitting you're upset. Say, *'I think you know I was really looking forward to being accepted for this position and it has upset me that I wasn't chosen. Can you help me determine what I'm missing in my background that's keeping me from being promoted?'*

He'll feel he's somewhat off the hook because you're discussing your failings, not questioning the decision. If he says, *'The other person was just better qualified than you,'* your response should be, *'Could you be more specific about the qualifications that are necessary for the job?'* After he has pointed out the qualifications, paraphrase what he has said and add, *'I have that kind of experience - in fact, I have more than you've said is necessary for that position, so I guess that isn't the problem.'*

He'll have to admit you're right. *'No, I guess not. You have seven years' experience in that area.'* (You know that George, who got the job, has only five years' experience. Don't throw this at the supervisor - store this information for later.)

Next you ask, *'What other kinds of qualifications were necessary for this position?'*

He may suggest some additional type of knowledge or experience and your reply might be: *'I don't think that's a problem either.'* Here you would give further facts showing that you have these qualifications as well (assuming you do). In short, keep giving factual reasons why you don't think his explanation eliminates you as a candidate. He'll try to pull out some plausible reason why you didn't get the job and he won't be able to do it.

At the end of the interview, you say something like, *'Well, I don't know where this leaves me, because it appears that, from what you've just told me, I was the best qualified for the job. As you stated, as far as experience is concerned, I needed five years' experience and I have seven. I know George only has five. As far as education goes, I have ... and I know George has only ... I'm still at a loss to know why he got the job and I didn't. What do we do now?'*

You've put this person on the spot. You've presented your facts in such a way that it can't be denied that you're right.

Many would say that all you've done is make the person angry. This may be so, but the supervisor will be angry because you're right and he's wrong. This may be the time to ask for an impartial person to be involved. If you're in a union environment, your steward could be called in to mediate. If it's a non-union environment, a representative of the Human Resources Department could be called in to solve the dilemma.

Another choice could be to mark time and leave the meeting with this comment; *'Well, it's unfortunate that this happened. I really feel upset, because I should have been given the job. Can I count on you to see that I won't be overlooked for the next promotion?'*

This type of approach is low-key without being wishy-washy. You keep your cool - and your temper - but also give yourself a better chance of being treated fairly in the future. It might put the company in a very difficult position to demand that they pull back the promotion they have already offered to George. If George had been given a written job offer, he would be able to sue the company. You may have let the company off the hook. They may even recommend you for a promotion in another department. In fact, that's one of the things you can ask them to do.

Would you feel comfortable doing it this way? I hope so. It's a win/win situation.

Try to guard against being overlooked for a promotion in future by making sure your boss knows what kind of career plans you have. Ask him or her to watch for any promotional opportunities that might help you get where you want to go. Otherwise, no matter how good your qualifications are, you might be overlooked again. The oversight may be unintentional - the result of a certain type of conditioning.

You need to make sure your employer recognises that you're a candidate for promotion. You might also talk to people in the Human Resources Department. Explain that you're looking for a promotional opportunity and ask to be kept informed about any suitable positions.

CONCLUSION

You now have many tools, techniques and ideas on how to handle difficult situations at work. These tools can empower you to deal with irate, rude, impatient, emotional, upset, persistent and aggressive people. These crucial people skills allow you to deal with all types of difficult people and circumstances. Learn these skills and you can't help but enhance your relationships with others.

Your proficiency in people skills will help you control your moods and keep you cool under fire. You'll start on the road to understanding why people interpret situations differently.

These techniques do work! But like any new skill, you'll have to use them unfailingly until they become spontaneous and automatic. If you do, you can look forward to being able to control how you deal with and react to others.

No longer will you allow others manipulate you or decide what kind of day you'll have by:

- Making you lose your cool;
- Forcing you to do things you don't want to do;
- Preventing you from doing what you want or need to do;

- Using coercion, manipulation or other underhanded methods to get their way;
- Making you feel guilty if you don't go along with their wishes;
- Making you feel anxious, upset, frustrated, angry, depressed, jealous, inferior, defeated, sad or any other negative feeling;
- Making you do their share of the work.

Because you've gained this control, your self-esteem level will raise accordingly. The more self-assured you are, the less stress and apprehension you'll feel, which will give you more stamina and enthusiasm. The rest is up to you. Use these skills and brace yourself for the success that will inevitably follow.

You'll find more techniques and ideas in my first book that has been an international best-seller since 1990:

Dealing with Difficult People – How to deal with nasty customers, demanding bosses and uncooperative colleagues

And other sequels:

Dealing with Difficult Spouses and Children;

Dealing with Difficult Relatives and In-Laws.

You might also be interested in my bullying sequels entitled:

Dealing with Workplace Bullies - Society's Corporate Disgrace!

Dealing with School Bullies – Society's Educational Disgrace!

Dealing with Domestic Violence and Child Abuse – Society's Judicial Disgrace! and

Retirement Village Bullies

BIBLIOGRAPHY

Killinger, Barbara, *Workaholics - The Respectable Addicts;* Key Porter Books, Toronto, 1990

Tannen, Deborah, *You just don't understand; Women and Men in Conversation;* Morrow, 1990.

Uly, William, *Getting past No;* **Negotiating with Difficult People;** NY, Toronto, Bantom Books, 1991.

www.ingramcontent.com/pod-product-compliance
Lightning Source LLC
Chambersburg PA
CBHW051635170526
45167CB00001B/201